mission-shaped
spirituality

mission-shaped
spirituality
the transforming power of mission

susan hope

Seabury Books
NEW YORK

Cover image courtesy of Thinkstock
Cover design by Laurie Klein Westhafer

Library of Congress Cataloging-in-Publication Data

A catalog record of this title is available from the Library of Congress.

ISBN 978-1-59627-129-6

Originally published in England in 2006 by
Church House Publishing
Church House
Great Smith Street
London SW1P 3NZ

Published in the United States in 2010 by
Seabury Books
445 Fifth Avenue
New York, New York 10016

www.churchpublishing.org

An imprint of Church Publishing Incorporated

Printed in the United States of America

Contents

Series introduction

In adopting and commending the *Mission-shaped Church* report, the Church of England took an important step forward in its understanding of God's mission. It is a journey full of opportunities and challenges, and one which opens up new questions. This series of titles is designed to resource thinking, reflection and action as the journey continues.

Each title in the *Mission-shaped* series considers how the principles presented in *Mission-shaped Church* can be applied in different areas of the Church's life and mission – in work with children and young people, in rural areas, in the parish church and in the area of apostolic spirituality. What perspectives and inner values are necessary to be part of a mission-shaped Church today? These areas were touched upon in the MSC report but are now explored in more depth.

All the authors write with the benefit of years of practical experience. The real-life case studies and practical examples they provide are designed both to be inspirational models of ministry and mission and to be adapted by the reader for their own context.

The examples cited include both 'fresh expressions', developed as a response to the culture of a particular group of people, and more traditional models, reflecting the fact that 'there are many ways in which the reality of "church" can exist'.[1] This series is firmly committed to advocating a mixed economy model for the Church of the future.

---

[1] Archbishop Rowan Williams, from the Foreword to *Mission-shaped Church*, GS 1523, Church House Publishing, 2004.

Foreword

Knowing God and being known by God makes a difference to the whole of life. Once you have caught a glimpse of God somewhere, you can't help looking for God everywhere. This impact – the impact of Christ in people's lives – gave birth to the Church. For the Church, in all its many manifestations, is that group of men, women and children whose lives have been turned around and centred on Christ. This impact continues to give birth to new ways of being the Church today. This intuitive knowledge that we need to live and share what we have received is the authentic mark of a spirituality shaped by mission that is God's missionary desire to be known and to make a difference in the world.

Susan Hope calls this an apostolic spirituality. We give from the overflow of what we receive. And we go on receiving. We know that we can do nothing unless we carry on abiding in God, allowing his life and energy to shape our lives. 'Go on being filled' is what Paul says to the church in Ephesus (Ephesians 5.18).

This book arises out of the deep well of Susan Hope's own abiding in God and the work she has done to encourage and facilitate the mission of God's Church. It leads us on what she calls 'an apostolic adventure'. We are encouraged to take the risk of allowing the gospel to shape fresh expressions of Christian community. We are also urged to remember that the mission belongs to God. For it is God's Church, and it is God's spirit – and his great love and faith in us – that will inspire and resource us.

Stephen Cottrell
Bishop of Reading

Acknowledgements

Unless otherwise indicated, Scripture quotations are taken from the Holy Bible, New International Version, copyright © 1973, 1978, 1984 by International Bible Society. First published in Great Britain 1979. Used by permission of Hodder & Stoughton, a member of the Hodder Headline Group. All rights reserved.

Extracts from the Aidan Liturgy and from the Daily Office are reproduced from *Celtic Daily Prayer*, HarperCollins, 2000, by permission of the Northumbria Community.

About the book

Sometime towards the end of the last millennium, the tide of the churches' mission in England seemed to turn. The water was still a long way out, but nevertheless something had changed. There was a fresh wind blowing. Parts of the Church seemed to be waking up, getting ready. People were talking about mission again, but in a different way. It was as though they were excited about it, as though it was all fresh and new. And this was right across the Church, throughout the different traditions and denominations. It wasn't wholesale, but patchy, a bit like rock pools filling up while the main tide is still some way out. And this tide of mission has continued to make its way in. It's been accompanied and encouraged by various publications on mission and evangelism, including, in the year 2004, the publication of the Church of England report *Mission-Shaped Church*[1] as well as by a shared Anglican–Methodist initiative to support part of the Church-in-mission-mode, currently known as *Fresh Expressions*.

Of course, the tide had probably been turning for some time before we noticed. Other events, further back, will have assisted it. Even the often-maligned 'Decade of Evangelism' in the closing years of the millennium can be said to have had an effect. We learned a lot in those years and we probably wouldn't be where we are now without it. Further back from then, in 1945, was another report *Towards the Conversion of England* with its urgent analysis: 'There can be now doubt that there is a wide and deep gulf between the Church and the people.'[2] Who knows what impulses flowed from this? I suppose if we went far enough back we'd arrive at the Early Church and at the outpouring of the Holy Spirit for the missionary task. Because it seems likely that it is, in fact, the Spirit who is the initiator of this present tide – and that our task is to try to go with him, surfing in on the waves.

This book has been written for anyone, of whatever denomination, who finds themself caught up in this present tide – or wanting to be. It might be a useful tool for PCC members, or leadership teams, as well as for clergy. It is an attempt to get at the inner workings of what happens to us when we go in mission, of what is going on inside us, of who we become when we start going – and of how this present tide might just change us, and change the Church. It's more of an aid to reflection than a 'how to' book and its purpose is to address the internal dynamics of our church life and our individual life: to ask questions about who we are – and who we are becoming as we respond to the present tide. It's not so much a book of answers as a book of questions and, if it works at all, it will work best where its contents are chewed over, argued over and prayed over. It is also full of contemporary stories of mission which, it is hoped, will trigger responses in those who read and reflect upon them.

Defining the terms

A brief word should be said about how the words *mission*, *evangelism* and *spirituality* are being employed in this book. A definition of *mission* quoted in *Mission-shaped Church* encompasses something of the breadth of it:

> God's missionary purposes are cosmic in scope, concerned
> with the restoration of all things, the establishment of shalom,
> the renewal of creation and the coming of the kingdom as
> well as the redemption of fallen humanity and the building of
> the Church.[3]

It is important for the purposes of this book not to narrow the definition down to 'the work of the Church' but to keep holding to a sense of mission as moving out from the Church towards the other, towards the outsider. I make no apologies for using the word 'missionary', believing it to be an accurate and good word to define those who undertake the task of mission, and hoping thus to rescue it from the disrepute into which it has sometimes fallen.

For *evangelism* William Abraham's broad and deep definition as

> that set of intentional activities which is governed by the goal
> of initiating people into the kingdom of God[4]

highlighting as it does the communal and social intention of the gospel message, will serve us well, coupled with the simplicity and brevity of the straightforward translation of the Greek *euangelizomai* 'to announce good news'.

And for *spirituality* I have in mind my own definition of 'life lived towards God'.

From come to go

Luke 10.2,3

In 1999 Kerry died. She was just 18 and she had lived in nine different children's homes. She belonged nowhere and with no one. She had tried to kill herself several times in her young life. Her body was found in a wooded part of the hospital grounds. She had somehow managed to strangle herself with the laces from her trainers. A post-mortem revealed that she had also taken a large quantity of heroin.

On a bitterly cold night in 2003, just before Christmas, Adrian, a homeless youth, crawled into a council wheelie bin in Doncaster town centre and died of a combination of drugs and hypothermia.

Kerry and Adrian are only statistics to most of us – just two unknown youngsters who got lost along the way. But they are not statistics to God. Nor are the countless numbers of people in England who, for very different reasons and in very different circumstances, find themselves alone, or hungry, or restless, or empty, or without hope, or burdened with guilt, or trapped by compulsive drives, or just plain bored with money, leisure and celebrity culture. There are others among us who face serious and life-threatening illness, or the break-up of a marriage, the loss of a child, the struggle with sexual identity, and whole communities, clusters, people-groups – asylum seekers, schoolchildren, farmers, fishermen, wealthy suburbanites, teenage mums, young sophisticates, musicians, gamblers and sportspeople, health workers and students – all of whom have simply never heard the gospel of Jesus in ways that make sense to them. Many find themselves clinging, sometimes precariously, to a sense of identity quarried from snatches of community memory and shored up with a pastiche of half-remembered wisdom woven with contemporary advertising slogans, all packaged attractively in the designer dress and consumer culture of twenty-first-century Britain.

A defining word

To all these people, individuals and people-groups, at this point in our history, God requires his Church to go. Once, they came to us. For 1,500 years the Church in England has been a settled Church. The word 'come' could be said to have defined our mission as a Christian community. 'Here we are. Come to us – we'll baptize your babies, marry you, bury your dead. And if you want to know a bit more, if you're interested in the Christian faith, why not come to a confirmation group?' And so for years they've come. Not in droves but in a steady trickle, enough to keep the Church of England at least feeling that it was fulfilling its mandate to be the Church of the nation.

Yet clearly, increasingly, they are not coming to us. The reasons are complex and multifaceted, and have been well explored elsewhere. As the report *Mission-shaped Church* makes patently clear: 'The reality is that mainstream culture no longer brings people to the church door . . . Instead of "come to us", this new approach is to "go to them".'[1] What is clear is that the defining word for the Church and its mission has changed from 'come' to 'go'. Moreover, this 'going' cannot be interpreted narrowly, in a geographical sense, as though geography were the prime interpreter of incarnation, but in the broader, deeper sense of going to be with people 'how' they are, 'connecting with people's culture, values, lifestyle and networks as well as with their location'.[2]

What powers the mission?

But if we are to 'go' in mission, where is the energy to come from? What powers the mission? What kick-starts it? What massive impulse can propel us from being a settled community – a 'come to us' community – into being a community on the move? And what will keep us going when we find ourselves in for the long haul?

For here we are – British Christians at the start of the third millennium – with a message to pass on. It's a message that must be given in both word and action. It's just possible that nothing else matters as much as this one task. The report *Mission-shaped Church* is helping us to re-evaluate our methodology, to find new shapes and patterns that can assist mission and evangelism in a post-modern, post-everything world. But the impetus, the passion, the desire to re-engage with evangelism in our culture and time, the longing to pass on this one message – to do the task that has been given to us – where is that to be found? Is there such a thing as a 'spirituality for mission', a spirituality that will engender and support mission – an apostolic spirituality? If so, what are its characteristics?

A question of confidence

Further, given the assault on Christian confidence, from within and without the Church, where is confidence for the task to be found? What does apostolic confidence look like in an age such as ours, an age of uncertainty? Does the question of confidence not sit uneasily in our present context, where extremism and confidence in matters of faith are so often confused in the public mind? Can apostolic spirituality find a shape that can hold to a confidence in the gospel without doing violence to the sensitivities of an age that is more trusting of a truth-seeking than a truth-claiming approach? And if there is a Christian confidence that can work for our age, how can the whole Church be infused with it, so that the apostolate of the laity, as well as that of the clergy, can be liberated to become an apostolic people?

Journeying off the edge of the map

It is with these questions in mind that this book has been written. It is not its intention, or claim, to try to be the definitive guide on what is a vast and – as yet, for many of us – uncharted water. (Uncharted, because for the English Church, the idea of *missionary endeavour* to its own people is largely a thing of the long-distant past. Indeed, given that the main missionary movements towards the peoples of these isles were at the initiative of the Romans and the Celtic Irish, it could be argued that the English Church as a whole has never systematically and intentionally engaged in a missionary work to its own people.) Nor is this a book about the spirituality of unchurched people and the kinds of connections that we can make with them. That is an important issue, and some of what I've explored will have repercussions into that topic, but it is not the focus of this book.

What I've attempted to do is remind us of some of the underlying dynamics of the mission task and alert us to the kind of people that we may need to

3

become in order to do the job. But the book is not only about this. It's also an attempt to say that going in mission may start us off on an adventure that is enormously and joyfully life-giving for the Church and for ourselves, too. The wholly new context in which we find ourselves provides us as a Church with, potentially, some of the most exhilarating explorations that we may ever encounter. For essentially the spirituality of the English Church – of whatever denomination or tradition – is that of a settled community. Its liturgies, its way of organizing itself, its buildings, its synods, its financial arrangements, its self-understanding, have been formed and shaped through a long time of settlement. Who knows what the journey of mission will do to the spirituality of the Church? Might it not be that as we move out, we'll find something happening to the Church itself? How might our faith, our priorities, our prayer, our way of living towards God be changed through the journey of mission?

Stories from the front

This book could have been written in a number of different ways. One way would have been to look back to great missionary movements and missionaries of the past in an attempt to track threads of missionary spirituality. Another way would have been to work solely with the biblical witness. I've taken a different route. For *Mission-shaped Church* has highlighted some of the ways in which journeys of mission are being undertaken at present, and the Church of England and the Methodist Church are working together through the Fresh Expressions initiative to encourage and resource such journeys. What is emerging from these early journeys is *stories*: stories of attempting to interpret the signs, of trying to discern the leading of the Spirit, stories of grappling with inner uncertainty, of adventure and of joy, of blind alleys and cul-de-sacs, of the formidable rock faces of indifference and of resistance – in the culture and in the Church – stories of the long uphill climb, the steady commitment to the enterprise, and of sudden surprise views.

In making use of these stories, I wanted to try to look forward a bit from what is happening at present, and to ask if it is possible to discern, in the weave of these stories with some of the stories of the missionary journeys of the Early Church, the warp and woof of a fabric, the threads and shapes of an emerging pattern of apostolic spirituality. Is it possible, through these stories, to take note of markers, signs, pointers, which describe something of the formation of a missionary people? The stories themselves are, of course, fragmentary, small, partial. But they do offer us an opportunity to listen to tales from the front. Their random nature probably means that they are better described as 'soundings' rather than research. For all those whose stories have provided this book with its living content, I am grateful. And I'm most particularly grateful to my friends at the Sheffield Centre, who *are* doing serious research into current church planting and fresh expressions, and who have given me so much support, encouragement and friendship.

'Traditional church' and 'fresh expressions'

While much of the material in this book has been drawn from those who are working at fresh expressions of church, this is in no way to imply that 'traditional church' is not called to be missionary. I have also included, therefore, stories from the more traditional parish model of mission. It is vital that we do not allow a wedge to be driven between the two models: indeed, many newly planted churches and fresh expressions are directly the fruit of an acknowledged missionary heart within the traditional church. The advantage, however, of quarrying much of the research from 'fresh expressions', is that it is just that – *fresh*. There is a possibility that in the very rawness and unformed nature of some of these early experiences in mission, we may hear and see something more clearly: indeed, we may find that 'a word' is being spoken back from the front into the whole Church, a word that can bring life. It is the whole Church, in all its diverse forms, that is invited to become what it is – one, holy, catholic and *apostolic*. None of us is exempt from that call. Besides, who wants to be left out of such an adventure?

2 Called and sent

'When Jesus had called the Twelve together ... he sent them
out ...'

Luke 9.1,2

Back in 1999, I began to get restless. I was vicar of a steadily growing church
in urban-suburban Sheffield. We had a sizeable staff team, including an
administrator, a thriving parish centre, youth work, children's groups and
home groups. Weddings and funerals kept us busy, as did pastoral visiting and
church committees. Enquirers and fringe people were introduced to the
basics of the faith through various nurture courses and by participating in
the Christian community. There was a small but steady trickle of people
coming to faith. Things looked good, healthy, satisfying. Yet, for me personally,
something was wrong. I found myself pacing about in my study, feeling
increasingly trapped by the paperwork, by the demands of the computer, by
the rut and the rhythm of being a vicar. It wasn't that I didn't enjoy it, or feel
it was worthwhile. But something was missing. I'd lost something and I didn't
know what it was. Over some weeks, I began to feel an inner impulse that
grew steadily into a quietly burning fire of conviction – I had to 'go'. I had
literally to 'go'. But where? And how?

I started to strike out days in my diary ahead, writing 'go' across them.
On the day in question, I would put on my dog collar and take a tram up
to town. Once in town, I found myself walking around among the people
in the city centre, and in particular dropping down to squat beside those
who were begging. 'I've got half an hour – tell me your story: how did you
get from being born to this pavement?' This went on for some months. I
learned some important first lessons in 'going'. I heard some amazing stories.
I gave away some Gospels, and spoke about Jesus to a few people.
I bought some cups of tea for others. I tracked down the family of a girl
who'd lost touch with them. And then I began to notice something –
that on my journeys home I was bursting with joy. The thing I'd lost had
been found. And with it had come a new energy for life and for ministry.
It came through simply 'going'. I also began to notice something else –

that the going didn't have to be 'successful' to bring joy – it just had to be *done*.

Uncovering the fire

In this chapter I want to highlight one key factor that is frequently involved in the recovery of vision and being re-energized for mission. *Re-energize* is an important word. For it is the perception of many church leaders, both clergy and lay, that the fire of mission, the DNA, the heart of concern for the 'outsider', is often submerged beneath the demands and duties of daily parochial life. For many of us, the fire is almost extinguished and we forget who we are and to what we are called. And through forgetting, we lose confidence, so that the task of mission, when we do look at it, seems over-whelming, impossible, out of our range. It can feel like just more hard work. In fact, there is a particularly powerful inertia that operates among many churches with regard to the task of mission. From where we are, it looks well nigh impossible. It's as though we are seated in a comfortable armchair by the fire. It's a dark night. We've got to go out, but the more we think about it, the less we want to do it, and the better our excuses for not going.

No one ever really argues themselves out of inertia. There is only one way to deal with it and that is to exert a counter force – to push through it, to pull against it. As soon as we start doing that, the inertia begins to release its grip. My experience, small as it is, would seem to suggest that the fire of mission can re-ignite *through the act of going*. This is not to suggest that we are to rush out anxiously, as the latest fix for our common frustrations – that will lead only to exhaustion and disillusionment. But it is to say that going in obedience to our original call can assist in re-igniting what is at the heart of us: that fire of love, for God and the world, that is the driving power of apostolic spirituality – spirituality for mission.

Tackling the inertia is essentially *practical*. It is likely to mean, for clergy and laity alike, going and doing a piece of mission (perhaps a very small thing, like visiting someone who has been on the fringe of church for ages but who we don't really know) rather than spending yet another two hours at the computer, or tidying up the parish room. This will almost inevitably mean putting one thing down, neglecting it, even, in order to do something else. This can exert the kind of pressure on us that is suggested by Jesus' parable of 'the ninety-nine' and 'the one' (Luke 15.4). Talking about the issue of priorities as a PCC, being frank about feelings, and making concrete decisions about actions, can help to deal with the kind of guilt and uncertainty that leaving the ninety-nine can provoke in us.

Remembering what we are for and about

But how are we to know that 'mission' is our original call? *Mission-shaped Church* reminds us that 'it is . . . of the essence (the DNA) of the Church to be a missionary community', because of God himself 'whose mission as creator . . . is to bring into being, sustain and perfect the whole creation, and as redeemer . . . to restore and reconcile the fallen creation'.[1] We are called into a relationship with a sending God and the simple fact is that an encounter with the sending God seems to produce people who are sent. Moses alone in the desert, Isaiah burnt out before the throne of God, Simon after a night's unproductive fishing, Mary grieving in the garden, Paul breathing out threats and murder on a journey . . . each one meeting God, each one in some way healed or transformed, each one then sent to 'go and tell'. You could say that the meeting marks them for mission. They are branded, burnt, with the fire of God.

Personal but not private

An apostolic spirituality, then, is one formed in and through the encounter with God. That encounter conceives, sometimes quietly over a period of time, sometimes dramatically and immediately, the confidence that we are loved and forgiven. And it brings the knowledge that this love is for everyone, and that the news of it, and the reality of it, are to be shared. In a curious way, the knowledge that we know we need to share this love can be the mark of authentic encounter with God. I say 'can be' because when God meets with us, we are sometimes so broken by life and life's events that it takes a long time for us to be able to give God's love away to others. But, nevertheless, true conversion leads us eventually out of ourselves towards others. God's love is personal but not private.

Sometimes – quite often, in fact – as I travel around churches, I find myself wondering how many in our churches have yet to encounter the living God.

I wonder that, not because I'm looking out for evidence of some kind of 'God experience' but because substantial numbers of worshippers seem frankly uninterested in moving out towards those outside the church. Or, if not uninterested, they seem confused about why they should do it. I find myself wondering what is really going on. Of course, not everyone's like Gordon Crowther, leader of the Church Without Walls, in Stoke. Conversion and call came together for him.

> story
> story
> story
> story
>
> **Conversion and commission**
>
> My conversion as a student also constituted, for me, a commission . . .The biblical story from Genesis revealed a missionary thrust for the people of God, and my own understanding of gospel was established around 'sharing the good we receive', expressing the grace of God to others and living as witnesses to Christ and ambassadors of the kingdom of God.[2]

But, nevertheless, where there is a lack of concern for mission, might it be one indicator to us that we haven't truly heard and received the gospel for ourselves?

From the general to the particular

All of us are called by the missionary God to share with him in his missionary work. For all of us, that constitutes a 'general call': to be witnesses wherever we are, at work, in the parish, in our networks. It means, too, a 'general call' to each church to live out a witness in its locality by engaging in events and projects that will communicate the love of God to others. But, increasingly, clusters of Christians from all traditions are discovering a 'specific missionary call': a call to go to specific people-groups, or age groups. It is impossible to categorize this kind of call, for the way it comes and its outworking are as diverse as the number of people who are hearing it and responding. For some, it's like following a hunch – there is nothing very clear-cut – they just seem to be being led into a relationship with a particular group of people.

Beginning with friendship

Otto is a Methodist minister in Bury, who found himself in relationship with people with learning difficulties. Out of that relationship, and in conjunction with other local churches and clergy, a monthly gathering, which includes food and worship, has developed, on a Sunday, for people with learning difficulties and disabilities. Now over 50 people are gathering there, carers and parents as well – and coming from increasingly far afield in the Manchester area.[3]

For others, God's call is something that grows inside; they become 'pregnant' with a desire to reach street people, or young mums, or office workers.

The growth of a call

Mark Meardon, the leader of the youth church, *Eternity*, in Warfield, says:

Looking back it's strange to think about where I am and what I'm doing now. A shy vicar's kid with uncontrollable hair, God used me at school to see many of my friends become Christians and as I left home to go to university, my heart continued to long for the young people there. After graduation I went to Africa, still with a passion, but now also with a vision for Bracknell. I eagerly returned to see about setting up a youth congregation.[4]

In some cases, people are finding themselves propelled, prodded, catapulted towards people – through circumstances or through, at times, personal adversity. One couple I know began to open their home to street people because their son had been in prison and through that they began to come into contact with a whole cluster of people – hidden people who lived on the streets.

Lions and jungles – or art and snooker?

These experiences of discovering that we are 'sent' to particular people stand in the line of all true missionary endeavour. The odd, surprising and energizing thing for so many of us is that in the churches we have been used to hearing stories of people being called and sent to places far away on the other side of the earth – but now we find ourselves being specifically called to particular groups here in Britain.

Moreover, many of us would have reckoned that missionaries were unique kinds of people, one-offs, exceptions – the kinds of people who would happily shoo off a lion with an umbrella or travel alone hundreds of miles through the jungle. But now we are discovering that all sorts of people can be missionaries and that a combination of prayer, teamwork, enthusiasm, imagination and openness to the Holy Spirit can actually be really effective in communicating the gospel today. We're also finding that it's perfectly acceptable to let mission take a human shape rather than an ecclesiastical one, that the things we enjoy, like art or running or snooker, might just be doorways for mission, and that the ecclesiastical-shaped doorways that are 'mock-Gothic and pointy' aren't necessarily the only, or the best, way in.

story
story
story
story

Finding a call

'X' is an artist. Having been in full-time ministry for many years, and being committed to sharing his faith with others, he began to ask God again, 'What is it that you want me to do?' The search for the answer was a long one, taking him into struggle, into weeping and crying out to God for a way forward.

Gradually he sensed God questioning him. 'What do *you* really want to do with your one life that I have given you?' He began to see that God had given him all he needed through what he loved to do most – which was to paint. So the door began to swing open – a door that has led to his working as an artist among other artists, building relationships, listening to his fellow-artists, exploring the spiritual side of who they are and of their work.

He is there as an artist in his own right. He is also asking the question of God, as he listens, 'What are you doing in this person's life? How, if at all, do you want me to join in with what you are doing?' He is discovering, too, a new joy and freedom in who he is: 'As I step out, sharing good news through being an artist, I realize that this "call" involves fullness of life – for me. I'm becoming more the person he intends me to be. Instead of living with guilt about evangelism – "I should be doing ..." – I feel an amazing amount of freedom. In fact, I'm like a dog with two tails!'[5]

Energy and joy

To sum up, then, being conscious of 'calling', of what-we-are-for-and-about, is a key motif in apostolic spirituality. Several contemporary theologians argue for a rediscovery of the call to mission as a powerful means of recovery and renewal for the Christian Church. So Walter Brueggemann warns of 'that amnesia ... which causes the church to lack in any serious missional energy'[6] and Andrew Walker describes this as 'a surface problem which betrays a deeper malaise: we have forgotten who we are. As long as we continue to be forgetters and not rememberers of the gospel ... then no real missionary energy for our modern culture can be found.'[7]

Being forgetters and not rememberers has always been a temptation for the people of God. Forgetfulness leads to a loss of direction, and a consequent betrayal of our call. Lesslie Newbigin writes:

We can see that wherever the missionary character of the doctrine of election is forgotten: wherever it is forgotten *that we are chosen in order to be sent*, wherever the minds of believers are concerned more to probe backwards from their election into the reasons for it in the secret counsel of God than to press forwards from their election to the purpose of it, which is that they should be Christ's ambassadors and witnesses to the ends of the earth; wherever men think that the purpose of election is their own salvation rather than the

salvation of the world: then God's people have betrayed their
trust. (My italics.)[8]

If forgetting what we are for and about is a clue to loss of energy, could it be
that remembering, being and going can be part of its rediscovery? Apostolic
spirituality is, I suggest, at the core of what it is to be a Christian. It is the
inheritance of the Church and of each baptized disciple. It is an inheritance
that has the potential to release enormous joy. It is also an inheritance that is
realized through action. We are all called to bear witness to the Christ. And
it is highly likely that, as in so many other areas of faith, it is activated through
obedience: 'As they went, so they were healed . . .'; 'As they put their feet
into the water, the sea parted.' As my own small story illustrates, it is very
likely that the energy will be released through the going. Might it not be the
case that as the Church moves into mission, she discovers a massive internal
release of energy and of joy?

3 Living trustingly

'Even the very hairs of your head are all numbered. So don't be afraid ...'

Matthew 10.30,31

Bread-making

It's six years since Methodist minister Barbara Glasson walked through the streets of the centre of Liverpool, praying and puzzling over the apparent withdrawal of the Methodist Church from the city centre. It felt all wrong. With Central Hall closing, it seemed they had pulled out and away from the street people, away from the shoppers, from the world of business and commerce. Besides, with the regeneration of the city centre into urban dwelling spaces, increasing numbers of mainly younger people were moving back into the centre. 'We ought to be here, in the vanguard, getting ready for them – setting the trend, being here for them when they arrive, not pulling out,' she argued. It was the start for Barbara of a new mission call. It was going to lead her out of the traditional model of church-based evangelism, and into something wholly different – a mission and a ministry that has grown out of the simple act of bread-making together. It was a big risk. She didn't know when she began that from those simple beginnings of bread-making, of people standing around the table, telling their stories, and life experiences, would grow a community which wanted to pray, to worship and to listen to God.[1]

Leaving the safe and the knowable

Loss of missional energy is not the only reason why we need to know what we are for and about. The very 'sentness' of mission implies some kind of traversing of boundaries, a departure from the safe and the knowable, that will possibly involve a challenge to the core identity of the one who is sent. So, in the mid-nineteenth century, Hudson Taylor wrote to his sister of his final step in transforming himself into a Chinese:

> I had better tell you at once that on Thursday last at 11 pm I resigned my locks to the barber, dyed my hair a good black, and in the morning had a proper *queue* plaited in with my own, and a quantity of heavy silk to lengthen it out according to Chinese custom.[2]

This was not only a cosmetic change for, as his biographer continues:

> The change he had made after so much prayer was soon found to affect more than his outward appearance. The Chinese felt it, the Europeans felt it, and above all he felt it himself – putting an intangible barrier between him and foreign associations, and throwing him back as never before upon the people of his adoption.[3]

That this movement out from 'self' towards 'the other', a movement that is at the heart of mission, makes great demands and requires particular resources is apparent from the life of Jesus himself. The *kenosis*, the self-emptying, of the one sent from God found its final expression in the death on a cross. The journey that Jesus made from the baptism to the cross was marked by joy, energy, clarity of focus, friendship, conflict, struggle, the adulation of crowds, powerful preaching and encounters with evil, including structural evil, and the great battle of Gethsemane and Calvary. The Gospel writers make it clear that the journey was resourced and sustained from a source that Jesus knew to be the Father. 'The Son can do nothing by himself; he can do only what he sees his Father doing . . . I and the Father are one . . . Anyone who has seen me has seen the Father' (John 5.19; 10.30; 14.9).

Conflict and risk

When we look at the picture of Jesus in the Gospels, we might be struck by the way in which so much of his ministry apparently took place in the context of conflict and risk. The image of 'sure repose' might now be a little too Victorian and idealized for us, but it is nevertheless hard to deny that the Jesus of the Gospels has a certain equilibrium, a certain self-assurance, that allows for him to give himself to others, even in acutely demanding circumstances. And if we ask, 'Where did he get this from? What was its source?', one answer might be that he could be this person, he could give himself, even in a context of conflict, because he was deeply secure in who he was.

Know yourself to be 'beloved'

For backtrack to the baptism of Christ and what do we see? We see the Spirit coming down like a dove out of heaven. We also hear a voice – a voice that says, 'You are my Son, whom I love; with you I am well pleased' (Luke 3.22). This is the start of the public ministry, the kick-start to all that follows. And it is kick-started with a word, not about the mission, but about being a *son*, and being *greatly beloved*. And not only greatly beloved, but *greatly delighted in* – 'with you I am well pleased' – carrying not so much the meaning, 'I'm pleased with you (because you've done a good job/obeyed me/you've met my demands)' as, 'You delight me; I enjoy you; I like what I see; when I look at you I go, "Whoopee!"'

Discovering that we are deeply loved is a lifetime's work. The artist whose story we noted in the preceding chapter found that learning in a deeper way about God's love for him, having that love somehow imprinted in him, was all part of the search for his new vocation. It was a necessary part of the journey towards a new work. In the place of struggle to hear God, he began to realize that he was being invited to trust. 'You are my beloved. Trust me. Believe in me.' He now says of that time, 'I learned that I couldn't make anything happen. The deeply ingrained lesson about trust, about letting God lead me, is what I take into the mission field.'

It may surprise us to realize that the question of identity lies at the heart of Christian mission – that knowing who I am before God, knowing myself to be greatly loved, is essential for the minister of the gospel. This 'knowing' is, of course, not a static, fixed knowledge. The search for identity is just that – a search, a journey, which takes a lifetime, and contains both delights and dangers on the way. Nevertheless, the starting place and the place of return, the default position, is always the I-Thou relationship and it is in that relationship that I am invited to find my primary meaning.

We can glimpse something of the importance of this relationship when we consider the parallel image of a young baby lying in her mother's arms, and remind ourselves that the child realizes her existence through the face of the mother gazing down at her. It is first and foremost because of 'the other', present in relation to her, that the baby knows that she *is*, that she *exists*. If the face smiling down at her is full of love, that message of 'being greatly loved' is laid into her core identity, providing a foundation of confidence, resilience and joy. Sadly, there are many in our world for whom the message was something else – coldness, indifference or hostility – and, worst of all, there are many for whom there was no face at all.

What it is vital for us to grasp as we consider apostolic or missionary spirituality is that the place of belonging with God (what Jesus called 'abiding') is the place from which all mission proceeds. It is our home in which we move out towards others, and it is as essential for Christian communities, for churches, to know this as it is for individuals. 'Knowing oneself to be greatly beloved' is thus one of the keys – possibly *the* key – to joyful, effective and resilient mission. Such knowledge, pressed into our present experience through the work of the Holy Spirit, both directly and through the reality of relationships within the Christian community, makes us increasingly secure in who we are before God – 'my son', 'my daughter', 'beloved', 'delighted in'.

All this – being secure in who we are, knowing that we are greatly loved – could run the risk of sounding like so much psychobabble, a kind of spiritual-izing of the Western preoccupation with 'self', if it were not for the healthy, salty, steely corrective of discipleship. We are to take up the cross and follow him. The demands of discipleship rescue us from the temptation to inhabit a kind of passive dependency in our relations with God. So worship, as it matures, is not just about being children and receiving from God, but also about our giving to him, and this giving is essentially marked by obedience. Nevertheless, this obedience is clearly *filial* obedience, the obedience of love, rather than the obedience of the dutiful citizen or the employee.

Living trustingly

It has been said that the greatest gift a parent can give a child is confidence – a gift to those who know they are loved. But being confident that we are loved by God, being confident in the gospel of God, is sometimes thought to be somehow unacceptable in today's contemporary climate. In fact, it has been known for confidence to be confused with arrogance, or a shallow superficiality. But let us examine what this authentic Christian confidence means. It doesn't mean holding a superficial, 'problem free' belief system.

The word 'confidence' is derived from the Latin word *confidere*, which means 'with trust'. For the Christian, this trust is rooted in, and finds its origin in, faith in the risen Christ and the reality of changed lives. But 'with trust' implies just that – trust – it suggests that it is perfectly possible for there to be a context of *uncertainty* in which the trust is exercised. 'Trust' is a word that applies to *relationship*, and this context of relationship allows for questions, argument, doubt, disbelief – it is a real relationship, not a fake one. It may be that, for many, there will be moments of great uncertainty in the journey of faith, that in times of darkness and trial and fear there will be the suspicion that to undertake the journey at all 'was all folly'.[4] We may not all languish, as did John the Baptist, in the darkness of an actual prison cell, yet, when all the circumstances seem stacked against faith, we may very well find ourselves crying out with him, '*Are you the one* – or are we to look for another?' It is interesting to note, incidentally, that the reply Jesus sent back to John was not an unequivocal 'yes' but instead invited him to listen and to look and to reflect and to make a trusting response on the basis of the testimony of his friends.

Authentic Christian confidence, therefore, is not about dogmatic certainties but about learning to trust. It's about daring to believe that in the face of many things that might suggest otherwise, God is good, faithful, just, true and knowable. Because Western culture sets a very high value on the search for authentic relationships, on what it is to be authentically human, Western people are likely to be attracted to the idea of a God who invites each of us into a real relationship, with its consequent passages of doubt and uncertainty as well as of joy and delight.

> The heart of Fresh Expressions for me is 'reality'. The more honest and vulnerable and real we are, the more people will want to be with us. We need to be real.[5]

The real choice is not between competing dogmas but about whether or not I choose to 'live trustingly', even, and especially, when the going gets tough. So part of Christian witness involves the willingness to be vulnerable: to let others see the struggles I have in my relationship with God, as well as the joys, to let lookers-on realize what the game is that I'm playing so seriously with this God, to let them stand at the edges as observers so that they might start to feel that they would like to play, too.

So how can we as English Anglicans, notoriously private about our faith, open up our relationship with God to the scrutiny of others? St James's Church, Doncaster, has started having a 'Barnabas Time' as a regular feature of its Sunday worship. This is a time for ordinary members of the congregation to share in their own words what God has been doing with them recently – during the week, during the last month – or what they feel he has been teaching them, or saying to them. These are not dazzling testimonies. They are often very simple stories about moments when God had to be trusted, moments when God was rediscovered. They often involve experiences of brokenness or failure. As such, they have the ring of truth about them. They serve to encourage others in the church – and they can have a significant impact on those who do not yet believe.

There are other ways of beginning to talk more freely about our relationship with God. Quite often we need to begin to share with one another *in* the church before we can have the confidence to share our faith *outside*. It can take time and patience to break down our natural reserve and talk about 'God-things'. To ask, 'What is God saying? What has he been doing among us since we last met?' can be a very helpful way of beginning a meeting such as a PCC. Even if the question is initially met by a blank silence, the long-term effect of such questions should be to help us to reflect on what might be going on underneath the surface of the church, to identify where God might be at work, and to have the courage to voice our feelings.

Facing the fear

Going in mission for some, if not for all, can be a fearful prospect. For a start, there may be real physical dangers, and those who engage in the dangerous places need lashings of good common sense, and practical support, if they are to fulfil their vocation. We also need to be ready for anything.

On a local estate

In early 2004 I went out prayer visiting with the Parish Evangelist on a local estate. On one particular road we were turned away at almost every door. A young woman with a baby answered one door we knocked at. We had a pleasant conversation and left her with a leaflet giving service times. However, as we were walking away I felt something whizz past my head and then heard the thud as an egg smashed on the ground beside me. The young woman and a young man pelted us with eggs until we were out of range.[6]

But there are other fears. Supposing I fail? If I'm the leader of the church and I fail, what will people think? Will I show myself up as 'no good at evangelism'? Supposing I get rejected? What if we've got it wrong? How are we going to speak about faith matters? Suppose we make a mess of it? And (in our present climate of anxiety about political correctness) what if we unwittingly cause offence?

Clearly these are issues that can be addressed by means of *training* at diocesan and district level. But they won't all be dealt with adequately through 'away days', or courses. For, primarily, these are issues that are lodged deep in the heart and the mind. They have been formed around our upbringing; they are about who we are, how we see ourselves, about our confidence, our personality types and our life experiences. We will probably find we need to work with, and through, them over a period of time and this will necessarily include risking some missionary forays, adventures, and mistakes.

Fear isn't in itself a reason for not doing mission. In fact, 'feeling inadequate, that we aren't able to do this' has very often been the mark of the true servant of God. Remember Moses, and Jeremiah. The good news is that fear shifts as we engage in mission. We begin to see that it really is unfounded, and that, far from rejecting us, many people, children, young people, adults, want to talk about issues of faith and appreciate the role of Christians in loving service and in community partnerships. Then we start getting freer of our fears and we begin to discover that 'going in mission' can be an agent of healing for us, too. And we find ourselves saying to other would-be-but-nervous missionaries who are standing shivering at the brink, 'Come on in, the water's lovely!'

Mission: not only for the young, the expert or the trendy

We were encouraged by a story of 14 elderly ladies in a small church who when they discovered that many of the children attending the school next door began the day without breakfast, started cooking and serving breakfasts in the church hall. After a while, concentration levels among children in the school improved, and so did relations between church and school. The head teacher became seriously interested and she and her husband eventually became Christians because of it.[7]

It doesn't take a lot to liberate us from fear, particularly if we are going out with others. And particularly if we know, deep down, that no matter what, we are each one of us deeply and dearly loved. In the fourteenth century, Julian of Norwich wrote:

> He did not say, 'You shall not be tempest-tossed, you shall not be work-weary, you shall not be discomforted.' But he said, 'You shall not be overcome.' God wants us to heed these words so that we shall always be strong in trust, both in sorrow and in joy.[8]

4 Seeing

'When he saw the crowds, he had compassion on them.'
Matthew 9.36

'Seeing' is part of encounter. 'Moses saw the burning bush.' 'Woe is me, my eyes have seen the Lord!' 'When Simon saw the great catch of fish.' 'I have seen the Lord!' 'The disciples were overjoyed when they saw the Lord!' 'Immediately something like scales fell from Saul's eyes.' This is the seeing of faith, which has God as its focus. It is a seeing that shapes us, just as Saul was shaped into Paul, and frees us from our small ambitions. It is also a seeing that cracks open the hardness of our hearts and beings to mould us into a new shape. 'If we were to live in a covenant with this passionate God,' remarks Moltmann, 'we would not become apathetic. Our whole life would be shaped by sympathy, by compassion.'[1] It is a seeing that leads to apostolic action.

For living in a covenant with the passionate, sending God means that we see not only him, but in another direction, too. There is another kind of seeing that is required for a truly apostolic spirituality and that is seeing the world, its beauty and its possibility and its woe. The eyes of Jesus are open all the time to this world. The words 'when he saw her . . . when he saw him . . . he had compassion on them . . .' run like a recurring piece of music through the Gospels. Does the seeing trigger compassion or does compassion cause him to see truly? Whatever the case, this compassionate seeing propels him out from himself towards others, in healing, in feeding, in restoration, in forgiveness, in works of mercy, in raising the dead to life.

This is a spirituality that burns – with love for God, with love for the world. It does not seek to drive a wedge between the 'material' and the 'spiritual' or set them up in any kind of competition. Bodies matter, too, in the seeing of Jesus. He is impelled out from himself towards all kinds of people in all manner of affliction. He manages to be deeply moved by what he encounters in the suffering of others without being so overwhelmed that he cannot also see God's creative possibilities in the given moment. His imaginative seeing can release new shapes from apparently fixed patterns.

It is all about opening the eyes and seeing what is there, but seeing it in a different way. He encourages us to see in the same way. 'Do you not say, "Four months more and then the harvest"? I tell you, open your eyes and look at the fields! They are ripe for harvest' (John 4.35). Which, being translated, may be something like, 'Don't always push the mission of the kingdom, the telling of good news, into the future – the realm of "One day ... when we've learned a bit more, when the church is stronger, when we've sorted out the roof, when we've got time to organize it" – look, open your eyes, you don't need to organize it or make it happen, it's now, today, there are opportunities right before your eyes!'

Contemplation leads to action

The willingness to see is the critical issue – 'willingness' because frequently it is easier to remain blind than to open our eyes to the broken places around us. Opening our eyes might mean having to get involved. It is easier to be like the priest and the Levite hurrying past the wounded man on the road, busy with their spiritual businesses. Both noticed the man on the road, and each chose to remain blind to all that was possible. It was going to be costly, it was going to be hard work, it was going to mean a change of plans. But when the Samaritan *saw*, really saw, the man, 'he took pity on him' (Luke 10.33). Contemplation, seeing deeply, seeing into the heart of things, has always been a component of spirituality. Here we see it leading to apostolic action.

The big issue

The Revd Dr Rich Johnson writes: I was rushing through Baker Street tube late for a meeting about how the Church can engage more effectively in mission and reaching our culture. I passed a man selling the *Big Issue*. I smiled an awkward, apologetic smile and rushed by, excusing myself with the knowledge that I had important stuff to do. Several paces past, I felt the Holy Spirit nudge me. 'What could be more important than taking the opportunity to be Jesus to someone in need?'

I stopped in my tracks, feeling stupid. Here I was, rushing to get to a meeting about being missional, about how we need to and can be Jesus to the messed-up world we live in, and yet failing to do that very thing. I went back, knelt down next to the man. He smiled a suspicious smile as I said something like, 'Hi . . . I don't want the *Big Issue*. To be honest, I don't read it. But let me pay for one, then you can sell it twice.' He replied, 'Oh, thanks very much.' I asked him his name. He replied, 'It's Gnasher.' . . . I noticed his tattoos, his size, his scars. This man was tough. I offered my hand saying, 'Good to meet you. Mine's Rich.'

As so often happens, at that point I didn't know what to say. Thankfully, Gnasher broke the silence. With a tear in his eye he produced a notebook in which he recorded how many people pass by and ignore him, and how many stop to buy a magazine, perhaps also finding a few minutes to talk. I guess it was a way of killing the pain of loneliness and boredom. He told me that 781 people had passed by that morning. He wasn't angry, nor upset, just matter-of-fact. I felt cut to the heart. I was so nearly number 782. No. I was number 782, but for the whisper of God in my heart.

I looked into his eyes and asked, 'What's your real name?' His voice softer, Gnasher looked back into my eyes, and replied, 'Peter.' Instantly I remembered the scripture I'd read that week on Jesus' grace for Peter. Peter the wobbly disciple, on whom he promised to build his Church. I looked back and said, 'I know a story about someone called Peter. Do you know what Peter means?' His reply, now more excitable, was 'Yes! It means the rock.'

I realized I stood on holy ground. I said, 'Yeah, Jesus promised to build his Church on the rock. Do you feel like a rock?' Peter said, 'No. I feel like a grain of sand.' My heart burned with compassion. This is mission. This is being Jesus. What more did

I need to know? How many meetings would get me to this place of understanding? How many more books on mission needed to be written before we just did it?

'Opening our eyes and seeing the fields' – really seeing them – is also essential for the kind of baptism of imagination that is advocated by *Mission-shaped Church*.[2] We need to open our eyes because unless we look in a contemplative, reflective and loving way at those cultures and people-groups that lie beyond the walls of the Church, we will be unable to see them truly. All we will see is our own 'gospel package', which we will be determined to shove at them without any kind of human meeting or dialogue. We need to be able to open our eyes so that we can learn the culture of the particular people-group to whom we are being sent and see in what way the gospel can be gospel for them.

Sunday morning in Asda

Fr Damian Heaney set himself a question. 'Where would a non-churched divorced male under 35 years old have a slack period in their week?' The answer was: after Grandstand and before the Pubs open – 6.30 on a Saturday evening. That's when he said Mass.

Then he moved parish and he and his wife asked a similar question. 'Which building do most people naturally go to?' The answer was Asda. The management was approached about the possibility of a weekly Sunday morning Mass at 10.00 am right in the middle of the 'way-in' concourse, followed by breakfast in the store. They all gave it 'thumbs up' and it was agreed that it could be broadcast over the store tannoy too, so staff could hear it too. 'Relaxed eucharistic hospitality was essential: any passing adult who wanted to receive would be able to do so.'[3]

A postscript to this story is that one day in 2002 Fr Damian went to visit a dying woman. 'What a coincidence it's you,' she said. 'I listened to you in Asda and said my prayers as I had my breakfast.'

We need, too, to open our eyes to see the quite extraordinary amount of suffering, pain and brokenness there is all around us – so that we can move out from ourselves to touch some of those broken places for God. *Mission-shaped Church* strongly suggests that the Church needs to repent for allowing our culture and our church to drift apart.[4] Unfortunately, for many of us the word 'repent' is tightly tied to liturgical action alone. But true repentance, as the report states, is about 'turning around and living in a new way'. Part of this turning around must be about turning away from ourselves towards the 'outside', and seeing what lies beyond our immediate churchy preoccupations, and then, when we truly see, asking ourselves and God, 'What, if anything, should I/we be doing about this?' For true sight must lead to questions about whether action is appropriate.

Dave Bookless is the UK leader of A Rocha, an international group of conservation projects with attendant Christian communities around the world. Before taking on that role, while working as a priest in Southall Diocese, he began to 'see' new possibilities for a large piece of wasteland, which led eventually to a project of community transformation.

Wildlife in a wasteland

In 1998, Dave began to notice what was under his nose. Overlapping with his parish was a wilderness of about 90 acres. It lay between strongly marked boundaries like major roads, a substantial brook and industrial estates. The Minet Site, so named after the family that owned it, had been sold to the council some years before. Classified as greenbelt, for decades it remained totally underdeveloped as a potential oasis among a densely populated urban area. Even on his first walk through he noticed the variety of bird life, decided to walk it regularly and completed a list of what he found . . .[5]

Freedom from anxiety

We also need to open our eyes because we are so often firmly convinced that there is no mission potential 'out there', when in fact it is all around us. It is not that it is not there, but that we can be blind to it. Churches and their leaders who are beginning to grapple with the kinds of issues raised by *Mission-shaped Church*, may find themselves worrying about how they are going to 'add mission' to their list of tasks, how they are going to find the time to commit themselves seriously to mission in a new way.

There are, of course, serious questions to be asked about priorities, about engaging with other people-groups, about resourcing fresh initiatives, and about sustainability. But at the root of this anxiety can be a false belief that mission is something that we initiate and therefore will require us to summon up a huge amount of energy, more than we have at present, as though the thing were all up to us. 'Opening our eyes and seeing' has a wonderfully liberating effect upon this kind of anxiety. It is not so much about our having to create opportunities for the gospel as about recognizing the opportunities that are there: 'Open your eyes and look at the fields! They are ripe for harvest ...'

Of course, special events can be significant, especially in terms of evangelism. And serious grappling with culture and people-groups and the question of how to reach them with the gospel is vital. But these are the icing on the cake. Its main ingredients are simple. They are the opportunities that the Holy Spirit initiates in our lives – in the queue at the post office, in the canteen at break, in the changing room at the gym, in the pub after work.

The lonely shopper

Jane was in the queue at the rundown supermarket on the estate. She noticed that the woman in front of her had, among other things, a bottle of sherry in her shopping basket. She saw tiredness on the woman's face. Jane reached out and touched the woman, and said lightly, 'I hope you aren't going to be drinking that on your own?' The woman burst into tears. That was exactly what she was going to be doing, just as she had been doing for a long time. Jane went back to her lonely flat with her, and listened to

> her story. The woman began to come to church and to find
> people who were committed to her. She found friendship, and
> she eventually found faith.

The task of an apostolic spirituality, then, includes the recovery of sight. It involves the spiritual discipline, the hard work, of maintaining a kind of double focus – on God and on those to whom God sends us. 'Love God . . . Love your neighbour as yourself.'

The seeing, of course, includes *attentiveness*:

> Attention to the mission context, or listening to the world,
> comes before discerning how the inherited Christian tradition
> works within it. Mission precedes the shape of the church that
> will be the result . . . listening to the context of the world
> shapes what emerges.[6]

Being intentional

The hard work and discipline of maintaining a double focus cannot be underestimated. It is unclear at present to what extent those who are beginning to make the journey of mission from traditional forms of church life into fresh expressions have been equipped and resourced for this 'long obedience in the same direction'.[7] But the stories from many of those engaged in Fresh Expressions have much to offer by way of assistance in the recovery of sight for the whole Church. What they can teach us is the importance of *intentionality*. For intentionality is about looking in a certain direction. It is about being oriented towards a particular group or place. It has a particular goal. It is fuelled by purpose. And there is something else about intentionality – as soon as people have it, and start using it, it tends to develop, to be something that increases rather than runs out.

But isn't 'intentionality' something that some people and churches have been blessed with – a sort of personality trait – whereas others just don't have it? My understanding is that intentionality can be developed on a very practical level, that it can be fostered by all sorts of groups and individuals – the mums' group, the PCC, the clergy person, the layperson at work. It starts with consciously 'training the eye' and that's when it begins to grow.

That growth may be a bit like this: first, we start believing that we need to see beyond church life, to see life 'outside'. So we start looking more thoughtfully 'outwards'. Then we find that, after a time, what we had previously seen in a blurry way, we begin to see a bit more sharply. Presently, a particular group of people comes into our line of vision. We find ourselves thinking about them, and praying for them. We begin to make individual contacts. Suddenly we find we are seeing them a lot more clearly. We also begin to see more clearly what, if anything, we might be required to do through these relationships. Life becomes much more clearly focused. It's as though all the way through the process a hand has been turning the lens of our sight so that we begin to see more and more clearly. And as the focus becomes sharper, so we begin to change.

---

story
story
story
story

How have you changed?

Here are some responses from young missionaries working across Sheffield in a range of Fresh Expressions when questioned about how 'going in mission' had developed them:

'I feel like my call has been increasingly awakened.'

'Seeing more people touched by Jesus has become a greater priority in my life.'

'Life has become very intentional.'

Another thing that can happen is that the more 'intentional' we become, the more focused on what happens outside church, the less importance we attach to 'church' as we have known. If, once we've journeyed outside a bit, we look back over our shoulders, we find that we see things from a very different perspective.

Mission-shaped Church reminds us that one of the long-term fruits of Christendom has been to skew the understanding of the Church's call towards the pastoral rather than the missionary. Beginning to see the ripe fields again can be hugely liberating because it begins to orient us to other goals than those of simply maintaining 'church'. We start making fresh discoveries about ourselves. We start realizing that there's something else to be doing apart from ordering new hymnbooks or organizing the summer fair. We also start getting free of what George Hunter, author of *How to Reach Secular People*, has called double myopia: 'Very few of the ordained clergy and other Christian leaders understand themselves, much less their congregations, as having inherited the work of the apostles to people who do not yet believe . . . They see neither their mission nor their mission field.'[8] Having our eyes opened is really good for us.

Following the Spirit into mission

But when the eyes are opened, what then? As Jesus himself saw, the needs are immense, and the workers few (Matthew 9.36, 37). Not all needs can be addressed, nor should they be. Not all inclinations towards mission will be fruitful. The apostolic person, like the apostolic Church, must learn how to follow the Spirit into mission. This is the seeing of faith, where the signs may be very small, as nebulous as a wisp of cloud by day, or sparks of fire in the night.

The Spirit in the vanguard

Stephen Cottrell inherited a Wednesday morning Eucharist drawing only ten. However, then it began to grow and some of them never came on Sunday. He confronted his own prejudices.

'While I was fighting a rearguard action to keep Sunday special, the Holy Spirit had danced ahead of me and was blessing Wednesday. Here without my properly realizing it was a church plant . . . that not only provided a place for a new worshipping community to develop, but also had within it people who felt so comfortable and nourished . . . that they were getting on with evangelising their networks and bringing people to faith.'[9]

All of us can be blinded by our prejudices and preferences. Too, there will be mistakes made along the way. There will be cul-de-sacs that will mean the retracing of steps and starting again. Learning how to do this, how to follow the Spirit into his mission, can never be fail-safe. And the Spirit can guide us in a variety of ways. It may be in the Celtic way of the early Irish missionaries – a way that is essentially responsive. We step into our coracle praying, 'Lord wherever the wind blows us, that's where we'll do mission.' Or it may be the Roman way, the kind of approach taken by Augustine when he landed in Kent with his 40 monks – a way marked by taking the initiative, strategic planning, moving out and then consolidating before moving on again. Joanne's story is a good example of a bit of Augustinian strategizing:

Beauty treatment

Joanne lives on a tough inner city estate in Sheffield. She's a young mum, a Christian and a beauty therapist. I bumped into her the other day. She told me that she'd been praying for the women who live in her road. She said many of them are broken and hurting people. 'I've been praying for them, and wondering how I can reach out to them with God's love. I've got a little idea. I thought I would invite one or two to my house for coffee and a free make-over. It would be nice to give some of them a bit of pampering – they need to be touched well, and with love. And I'll have my palm cross on the mantelpiece as usual, and be praying that I may be able also to tell them about how knowing the love of Jesus has changed my life.'

It is probably true to say that both models of mission – the Celtic and the Augustinian – are useful at different times and in different circumstances. After all, one is more right brain, the other more left brain – and we need both to operate well. But either way, our dependence is upon the Holy Spirit. And learning how to interpret what he is saying to us, how to see where he is nudging us, is a major task for apostolic spirituality.

One story of a new opportunity to do mission to young adults in the town centre of Reading grew out of a willingness to contemplate the real situation in which the Rector and the churches found themselves.

story
story
story
story

The city centre is changing

Suppose you led two town centre parishes. Neither church is very strong and one is very weak. St Laurence is attended by twelve mainly elderly people, all of whom travel in for traditional high church Eucharistic worship. St Mary the Virgin is the civic church and attracts 30–40 attendees. You look after both and dash from one to another on a Sunday morning . . . The second congregation looks viable, but is the first heading inexorably toward closure? At the other end of the high street, within a quarter of a mile is Greyfriars, a flourishing eclectic church, in the classic evangelical tradition with a team of leaders and workers and many hundreds of members. At the same time the town centre is changing fast. A large, brand-new shopping complex . . . is springing up. A quarter of a million shoppers a week will go through its doors . . . Themed pubs and clubs are clustering near the door of the weakening church . . . It seems as though words of the burial service are becoming true for the church, 'In the midst of life, we are in death.'

This is the position Canon Brian Shenton, the town centre Rector, found himself in as he sat one day for contemplative prayer in St Mary's. He had noticed the change of culture in the town. Ruminating on St Laurence Church, he found himself thinking, 'Let it run down, have a review, even if I lose my job – I must go out into the darkness and put my hand into the hand of God. This will be safer than a known way.' Willingness to let go was a genuine lever for change in this story. Humility and realism made possible what followed.[10]

Reading the signs

Of course, following the Spirit into mission does not mean that the outcome is always 'success' in our terms. The outcome for Joanne may not be quite what she expects. Or it may exceed her greatest hopes. It may be something that grows very slowly indeed. It may apparently bear no fruit at all. Nor are the signs always apparent. For those beginning to ask questions about the shape of ministry in Reading city centre, the journey to the answers has been slow. The way ahead did not become clear all at once. Some ideas that were thought possible turned out to be dead ends. There were big questions that could only be resolved, in time, by travelling towards them.

As we have already suggested, for the person or church moving into mission there are steep learning curves ahead. A nice little account from the missionary journeys of Paul illustrates this. He and his companions have been 'kept by the Holy Spirit from preaching the word in the province of Asia'. It is a useful and interesting exercise to reflect on how they worked this out. Could they not get across the border? Were they interpreting circumstances – or did they glean it through prayer? Had there been a word of prophecy about the direction they were to take? Or was it that their contacts had gone 'cold?'

They then find themselves travelling through the regions of Phrygia and Galatia and, next, try to enter Bithynia: 'but the Spirit of Jesus would not allow them to'. What happened? Did they not have the right visas? Were they stopped at some kind of border crossing? Or was this something they realized as they sat and talked and ate together? Perhaps they had had a very negative and hostile reception? Whatever happened, their interpretation is again that it is Jesus. So, they decide to head down to Troas. In the night Paul has a vision of a man from Macedonia, standing and begging him, 'Come over and help us.' They conclude that God is calling them to preach the gospel there – and off they go again! Would they have been able to 'receive' that dream if they hadn't already been trying one door, then another?

Free to fail

Mission-shaped Church sets a brave agenda for missionary endeavour among the churches in the British Isles. All the indications would seem to suggest that the report has caught the growing wave of mission that is currently gathering momentum among a great many different churches, denominations and Christian groupings. With skilful use, many of its recommendations can become, like a surfboard, the means of riding the wave of mission – and finding it an exhilarating ride. But learning to ride a wave doesn't happen automatically. And as the Church moves into engagement with mission, its spirituality must be such that it can weather the inevitable mistakes and failures. It must be allowed to fail, and to keep failing, to search and to keep searching, to make mistakes and pick itself up and try again. It needs to recognize that in this matter – in the missionary task to these islands – it has a lot to learn and to relearn.

There must be a freedom to fail. No skill is grasped without much practice, without much effort and trial and error. It would be foolishness in the extreme to assume that all the Church needs to do is to set off on the journey of mission and that by so doing all outcomes will be assured. The task of allowing the Spirit to make us once again 'apostolic' will not happen without our sometimes getting it wrong. It is hugely important that we should realize that we are all learners in this missionary task. No skill is learned without the doing and the redoing of certain basic things.

'I will make you fishers of people,' said Jesus to the fishermen by the lake – and he could have added to us, '*make* not *magic*'. The making of a missionary, and the making of a missionary church, is not accomplished by the wave of a magic wand or even by the intention to become what we are promised we can be, but by a long journey, with God as the prime teacher and the hard realities of the mission field as our classroom. The lessons along the way might well be painful. But as one young pioneer minister working among young adults in Bristol has put it, 'I'd rather fail trying, than fail to try!'[11] What kinds of lessons might we find ourselves learning if we can dare to open our eyes and start allowing the Spirit of God to lead us into mission? What kinds of adventures might lie ahead, and what kind of a Church might we become?

5 Take nothing for the journey

'Take nothing for the journey – no staff, no bag, no bread, no money, no extra tunic.'

Luke 9.3

Travelling light

In this chapter, I want to explore some of the issues of spirituality that lie behind the Lord's instruction to travel light on the missionary journey. Most biblical scholars, commenting on the limitation of luggage of the early missionaries, agree that its primary role was two-fold.[1] First, it ensured that those who travelled out had to trust in God's provision. Secondly, the need for a place to eat and sleep, the search for 'the person of peace', propelled them into a necessary relationship with the people to whom they were sent. We shall examine these points in a moment.

We might also find two other strands of meaning woven into this instruction to travel light. Both are, perhaps, discoveries, or rediscoveries, of the Church in our time. One can be said to be rooted in the knowledge that in the past, cultural imperialism has frequently operated whenever missionaries have gone out into other cultures. We are now wary about imposing our culture along with the gospel. And this applies not only to those exporting the faith outside these shores. One of the central themes of *Mission-shaped Church* is that 'church planting that sets out to serve an identifiable group, culture or neighbourhood cannot begin with a clear understanding of what form or expression the resultant church may take'.[2] True mission, wherever it takes place, requires 'double listening'. This means that while the identification of mission goals is legitimate, and will in some cases be vital, the shape of the Christian community that may result from the missionary journey must not be predetermined. This principle holds particular challenges for the ones who are sent, particularly when 'church-as-we-know-it' has been deeply ingrained from childhood. For some of us, thinking outside the box about other ways of embodying the message of Jesus can be deeply unsettling.

The second strand is related to this idea of refusing to predetermine outcomes, and is perhaps even more contentious. It is what might be called an 'empty-handedness' about the presentation and proclamation of the gospel message itself. We shall return to these two strands later in the chapter.

Trusting in God's provision: where the rubber hits the road

To state that a two-fold dependence – upon God and upon those to whom we are sent – for our material needs, is potentially uncomfortable for twenty-first-century mission is perhaps to state the obvious. It really is where the rubber of our faith hits the road of reality. What might not be quite so obvious is the suggestion in the Christian tradition that money and possessions, 'Mammon', may actually hinder the work of mission, that, in fact, selling out to materialism may limit spiritual effectiveness – or, conversely, that the holding of possessions lightly may lead to blessing in other ways. Is it just coincidence that sees lightheartedness about ownership of goods as a context for healing and effective evangelism in the stories of the Early Church? 'No good asking me for silver and gold – haven't got any. But I will give you what I have – in the name of Jesus of Nazareth – walk!'(Acts 3.6). 'No one claimed that any of their possessions was their own, but they shared everything they had. With great power the apostles continued to testify to the resurrection of the Lord' (Acts 4.32-33).

The 'danger' of money and affluence has always been around in Christian teaching. Jesus started it, of course. In the days of early Christian history, the Church's spiritual leaders had warned of the power of wealth to destroy the soul and relationships. Disciples were urged to go beyond the demands of the Law (i.e. tithing) because the fear that led to accumulation had been addressed and they had discovered themselves to be free.[3] The issue of freedom is a crucial one, especially for Christians involved in mission to a culture for which consumerism is the dominant force. Evangelism for such a culture means an invitation to 'change gods' and, as we see graphically illustrated in the story of the sons of Sceva (Acts 19.13-16), those who seek to minister Christian freedom must themselves be free. It really is, again, where the rubber hits the road. 'You cannot serve God and Mammon,' says

Jesus, trenchantly. Justin, in his day, remarked how pagans were turning away from violence and tyranny 'because they were drawn to Christians as people whose lives were distinctive and free'.[4] I wonder if twenty-first-century Western Christians are living lives that are clearly distinctive and free as regards possessions?

I guess we have all got something of a journey to make on this, and it might be that moving in to mission helps us to travel farther. Mission can assist in the freeing process by refocusing us and reordering priorities, drawing out resources that we didn't know were there, as this account by someone 'looking back' suggests.

story
story
story
story

The narthex project

In the early 80s several people at St Thomas's, Wincobank, a small urban church in the Diocese of Sheffield, believed that God was going to grow the church – that more people were going to come – and so the facilities we had needed to be improved and expanded.

Several of us prayed with the clergy and the idea of the narthex project was formed. It was an exciting and wonderful day until the day the builders came in and stripped the area and dug out the foundations. Staring into that deep hole with the realization of all the money we still had to raise was a shock. We learned to lean on God in prayer and fasting for each instalment of money paid to the builders. Some of us were called to trust him enough to give sacrificially – one young woman, married with three children and not herself a wage earner, brought £3, which was all she had of her 'own' money, and gave it gladly – while others were called to trust him with the well-being of our families while we took on part-time jobs and contributed the money we earned. All the bills were paid in full and on time.[5]

Trusting in God's provision: living by another story

The likelihood is that money and possessions can also be a barrier to mission through the issue of credibility. In 1980, an international consultation on simple lifestyle agreed that:

> The call to a responsible lifestyle must not be divorced from the call to responsible witness. For the credibility of our message is seriously diminished whenever we contradict it by our lives. It is impossible with integrity to proclaim Christ's salvation if he has evidently not saved us from greed, or his lordship, if we are not good stewards of our possessions, or his love if we close our hearts against the needy.[6]

If it is true that 'evangelism means inviting people into these [biblical] stories, as the definitional story of our life ... thereby authorizing people to give up, abandon, and renounce other stories that have shaped their lives in false or distorting ways',[7] how much attention should the local church give to this issue as it moves more strategically into mission? Giving some serious attention to the place occupied by money, finance and possessions within our common life may highlight some important issues for us. It would not be the first time that God's people have discovered that it can seem more comfortable to live in slavery in Egypt than to walk in freedom to the land of promise. The osmotic character of the Church in relation to 'the world' means that it is highly likely that we, too:

> come with our imagination already saturated with other stories to which we have already made trusting (if unwitting) commitment ... By their constant retelling (through propaganda and advertising, or even through parental inclination), we have come to take these stories for granted and as 'given'.[8]

Mobile church

One consequence of buying uncritically into the values of having, and highly valuing, possessions and positions that bind us to other allegiances, is that their place in our lives may severely limit our mobility and our ability to follow. The man Abram, though elderly by today's standards, and settled, with many possessions, was still free enough to obey the call of God (Genesis 12.1-5) whereas the rich young man in the Gospels found himself, when the call came, unable to follow (Matthew 19.16-30).

What do you need to 'be church'?

On Monday 27 March 2000 the church building of St John's Chapeltown, Sheffield, was declared unsafe and closed by the insurers. The church found a home in the local community centre. The vicar and the churchwardens, wearing hard hats, went round the old building salvaging anything that was needful. But what was needful? What do you need to 'be church'? That was the question. In the end, they packed up two plastic boxes. One box contained stuff for communion – some pottery communion chalices (they left the silver as being unsuitable for the community centre), the communion books, a fair linen cloth, a couple of small candle holders. The other was for baptisms, with the orders of service, candles, a pottery bowl, a small towel . . . Along with the two boxes they took a small communion table and the paschal candle stand. Everything went into the back of the van and there it was – mobile church!

What are some of the practical issues that church leaders might find themselves addressing here? Some issues go back to that nitty-gritty fact of 'knowing ourselves to be loved': that when God's people are confident about their relationship with him, it has a knock-on effect on their over-anxiety about Mammon. As one diocesan secretary was heard to remark concerning finances in his diocese: 'I've come to the conclusion that when people know Jesus, they give – and when they don't, they don't!' Then, too, it can be important for the PCC to take a lead in acts of faith regarding the church's attitude to money: regularly tithing income, providing goods and services free of charge, taking on a building project, making sure that 'finances' do not dominate the agenda of their meetings, sharing resources with other churches in the area. And we always need to check that as a church family, we aren't being 'mean'. Meanness is very often the fruit of fear, whereas generosity is one of the outstanding marks of faith. The church that can give away time, money, hospitality, good food and drink – even when it is not materially rich – is a warm church, one marked by grace. And it's a church that others like to be part of.

How might the Christian Church be affected as it moves out in missionary obedience 'taking nothing for the journey' – or at least 'travelling light'? Is it not likely that an apostolic spirituality will be marked by mobility, by freedom and by the joy of living by another story, in increasing material dependence upon God? And might it be that, as a consequence, the Church finds itself to be freer, more joyful, more dependent, more trusting?

Limited resources lead to connections

The second missionary principle underlying the instruction 'take nothing for the journey' is this – that dependence, being without, lack, lead to a position of deep connectedness to the community to which the missionaries are sent. 'Taking nothing' means that they are dependent upon those to whom they go. Because they have limited resources themselves, they are to search for the person of peace, and to lodge there – and in so doing they lock their own small community on to another one – and that means that there can be what postmoderns might term 'flow'. They are not to set up a mission compound that keeps them separate in their self-sufficiency from those to whom they are sent: no – they are to live with them, to share their lives with them, thereby making natural channels down which the water of the gospel can flow.

Apostolic spirituality is not set apart from the world, but finds itself deeply integrated into the networks of human relationships that make up our many worlds. It has to learn how to be unafraid, and it has to be prepared to be scrutinized at close quarters, to be shown up, to be 'read', to be accessible. The locking-on of the Christian community to the community of the person of peace, the willingness to be close, to be friends, the refusal of any kind of power or pedestal, being open to receive as well as to give – all this marks out the depth and quality of a truly apostolic community. 'Will you give me a drink?' says Jesus to the woman at the well (John 4.7), thereby placing himself in a relationship of mutuality with her. Recognition of mutual interdependence, of shared humanity, prepares the ground for dialogue, for true meeting.

story
story
story
story

Street supper

Back in 2001 the church of St Mary, Stainforth, near Doncaster, helped start a local Drugs Focus Group by helping bring together local health workers, social workers and family members. Two years later, in 2003, after a lot of lobbying they managed to obtain funding to provide a full clinical and rehabilitation drugs project in the community of Stainforth. Within one year over 100 local heroin users had voluntarily registered. At the end of 2005, an application was made for funding to expand the project to employ two full-time alcohol workers. The project has now been given the name STAND (**S**tainforth **T**ackling **A**lcohol '**N** **D**rugs) a name suggested by a client of the project in a competition they ran. But it's also a name with great gospel / New Testament echoes.

Nearly five years after the genesis of the project a new possibility emerged.

Through our links with STAND, the church was approached by the 'client rep' at the beginning of December 2005 with a special request. We were asked if we could provide a soup kitchen over Christmas for the homeless clients of the project. A lady in our church with a wonderful gift of hospitality, a great cook and organizer, enthusiastically offered to prepare two full cooked meals on two nights a week, Wednesdays and Sundays at 5.00 p.m. She offered to do this for a couple of months at least, and for all clients of the project affected by deprivation and not just the strictly homeless. The client rep was delighted to accept this offer. Our PCC (church council) agreed for the church kitchen and vestry to be used for the new venture although the meals are mainly

cooked at the lady's home because the church kitchen was only adequate for heating things up/keeping them warm. The PCC also voted £200 from our Community Outreach Fund, a fund we had specifically set up and given into for outreach projects. Church members also made gifts directly to the new venture.

We started on Sunday 18 December, the night of our Carol Service. At first only two clients of the project came but after a few weeks word got around and the numbers grew. Three months later we are now regularly serving full cooked meals for around 15 guests on two evenings a week, from a pool of around 25, including several young children of the guests who they bring with them. We try to make each meal a special occasion with a tablecloth and candles. The team of volunteers have built up warm relationships with the clients and there is a lovely atmosphere.

The relationship is proving to be one of mutuality: the church is receiving as well as giving.

The generosity of the venture, the principle of simply giving with no strings attached, and the down-to-earth friendliness shown by our volunteers, has generated a lot of goodwill. When a problem arose with vandalism to equipment our builders had parked outside the church, two of the Street Supper guests offered to sleep outside overnight to keep guard. The local Business Forum have also recently heard about the project and have responded generously, inviting us to write to them to obtain funding to help with our food costs and enable the venture to continue.

For some people the project is providing an opportunity to reconnect with issues of faith.

One or two of the guests have a faith background from time they have spent in residential rehabs. Others have asked about our bi-monthly bereavement service and whether they can light a candle in the church. We have recently started a 40 Days of Purpose spiritual growth course and one of our guests has taken a copy of *The Purpose Driven Life* to read.[9]

Take nothing ... go and inhabit

The third mission principle that we might suggest underlies 'take nothing for the journey' is that of not taking too much of our own ecclesiastical baggage with us. 'Network church encourages a "go and inhabit" approach; gospel and church becoming a reality among the variety of ways people are living,' say the authors of *Mission-shaped Church*. It is the case, of course, that none of us goes totally empty-handed, as the report continues:

> The planters – here understood in the simple, generic sense of those involved in the starting and sustaining of further and fresh communities of faith – carry with them an existing understanding of the faith and of church. They do not come with empty hands, but the next task is to have open ears. Attention to the mission context, or listening to the world, comes before discerning how the inherited Christian tradition works within it. Mission precedes the shape of the church that will be the result when the seed of the gospel roots in the mission culture.[10]

Travelling without too much ecclesiastical baggage is likely to prove a challenge for any of us.

How we went and had to let go

Laurence and Beth Keith write:

In September 2003 we were given the leadership of a cluster in St Thomas' Church, Sheffield. By Christmas, it

became obvious we were not called to sustain the Christians in the group, but focus on the de-churched, or post-Christians, we were in relationship with. Most of these were ex-St T's people, and quite post-modern, who had found their time at St Tom's to be difficult. So we began a journey we were not expecting.

Coming from St Tom's, we were rich in the language of lifeshapes (a discipleship course run by the church). Most of the people we had could not bear it, as they found it proscriptive, restrictive or oppressive. We still believed in the values, but had to communicate and disciple without ever referring to the shapes, creating our own culture of acceptable spiritual language.

When it came to worship, they realized that they had to do a rethink:

Needless to say, one man and his guitar would be scorned! The main thing was Friday Night Film, where someone would put on a film, explaining why they had chosen that film at the start. This led to open discussions, non-prescriptive and non-formal, which were good for community, and sometimes directly got to God, but not often. We didn't really nail this one, but in terms of community meeting with God, the only overt worship was contemplative, either silence or led silence, reading Bible passages and asking God to speak. They were open to the Holy Spirit, but not so open to the role of the priest (leadership in worship). Interestingly, some weren't Christians and still aren't and have never considered us their leaders. Yet they were still happy and able to engage directly with God. This was an obvious challenge to our concept of how the Holy Spirit works!

And finally their lifestyles were unexpectedly changed:

Many Christians have many meetings but it was not
appropriate to do that. So, we became poker players,
football players and film buffs, because that's where the
community found life. None of these things had previously
interested us, but we take the opinion that we all learn from
each other, rather than the top down model where
'everyone you know who isn't a Christian, you are
discipling'. Our lives have been truly changed by these
people, and though we stopped officially meeting (it was a
temporary waystation in Alan Jamieson's language), some
have re-engaged with the wider church and some have not,
but nearly all have worked through pain and doubts and are
disciples of Jesus. Some of them have become some of our
closest friends.[11]

The 'nothing' that we are to take as apostolic people might include, then, the
'nothing' of presuppositions, of preconceptions, of prejudging what shape the
church will take. It is the refusal to engage in a kind of cultural imperialism,
the refusal to impose a vision of how church life and worship should be
expressed.

Freedom and trust

It takes a certain amount of freedom and trust to enable the church to be
formed by the evangelized community itself. Vincent Donovan's experience
with the Masai in the 1960s, when he resisted the temptation to 'take
church' as well as Christ, was to develop his theory of 'taking nothing'.
He says:

> Church-planting and church-establishing have often been used
> as descriptions of a missionary's task. But such descriptions
> can be misleading since they necessarily imply a kind of fixed
> and predetermined outcome to the preaching of the gospel.
> Because a missionary comes from another already existing
> church, *that* is the church he will establish. I think, rather, the

> missionary's job is to preach, not the church, but Christ. If he
> preaches Christ and the message of Christianity, the church
> may well result, may well appear, but it might not be the
> church he had in mind.[12]

Coming as he does from a highly sacramental community, Donovan's journey of discovery among the Masai should be of particular interest to those groups in the historic churches that argue that because *Mission-shaped Church* not only lacks, but overlooks, a developed ecclesiology, its central tenets are unacceptable and unworkable for more sacramental Christian communities. He illustrates graphically how 'church' is discovered, uncovered almost, through sowing the seed of the gospel in a given community – leaving the response to be worked out by the indigenous community.

One of the most valuable lessons from the work of Donovan has to do with the freedom we need to trust people to make their own responses to the word of the gospel – which must include (as we have already noted with the rich young ruler) the decision not to follow. Such interior freedom in the apostolic person is able to provide 'spaces of generosity' in which seekers and searchers are able to feel at home, including when they are doubting and questioning. It is an approach that is non-manipulative – essential in a culture wearily aware of sales techniques and abuses of mass evangelism. It puts the missionary into the power of the other, and in so doing removes from the action of evangelism all possibility of coercion or force, leaving the one hearing the good news with the freedom to respond or not.

In essence, having the freedom and trust to let people work things out for themselves signals the belief that the work of mission and evangelism is God's work. If we really believe in the power and presence of the Holy Spirit, then we can have a certain lightness of approach that does not seek to 'make converts' but to proclaim truthfully, in word and deed, the good news as we have received it.

An empty-handed approach to proclamation

But what about the good news as we have received it? How can apostolic people say that they take nothing for the journey when they have a message to impart? Are they not travelling out already with the belief that Jesus is alive and that, therefore, Jesus is Lord?

As we have already stated, we recognize that we take something, that we have a history, a tradition, a faith – and it would be disingenuous to pretend otherwise. Perhaps 'taking nothing for the journey' at this point in the history of Christian mission could mean, then, a refusal to take the gospel as a 'package' – a package that is to be shoved at people, without dialogue, without debate, without negotiation and without recognition of 'the other'. Most of us will have had, at some stage, a doorstep visit from a member of a cult and will have experienced the sense of a package being presented without any possibility of dialogue, of negotiation, or of relationship. The package is to be delivered regardless of the intended recipient. One suspects that underlying such an approach there is likely to be a deep fear and anxiety on the part of the bearer of the package and a desire to get the job done.

I suggest, therefore, that 'taking nothing for the apostolic journey' means travelling light in terms of preconceptions about what might be discovered 'out there'. Taking nothing for the journey refuses to carry a package that is to be laid on people, regardless of who they are or what their circum-stances. It means going in a spirit of listening – listening to those to whom the journey is made but also listening to the Holy Spirit's answer as we ask, 'What's needed here? What gift of God's grace am I being required to give away? Is it an offer of prayer? Is it "the cup of water"? Is it a word about Jesus? Is it a word of consolation? Is it a touch – or an offer of a meal? Or perhaps they have something to give us?'

For people on the edge

It felt quite scary. We (at St Mary's) realized that we needed to follow up some of the visitors to our Christmas services: we'd tried before offering Alpha and *Start!* – but people weren't interested – it was all a bit too 'early': a set course seemed a bit too formulaic for where these people were, right on the edge. So we decided to offer an opportunity to listen to their questions. For me as the vicar, well, it was just the unknown. Who would turn up?

Would they ask questions that turned into a nightmare to respond to? Were there going to be masses of complicated pastoral and theological issues? How would it all work out?

What we did in the end was to offer two evenings – one to listen to the questions, and then an opportunity to put a Christian response to one or two of them. We were honest about 'where we were coming from'. We met in the church hall – started with drinks. We had tables for six nicely laid up. I opened with a five-minute introduction on how important questions are ('Did you know a four-year-old child asks, on average, 470 questions in a day?') – and that God values questions, too. Then there was about 40 minutes of everyone tucking into pizzas while talking about their questions. We had someone on each table jotting the questions down.

In the end, the second evening was devoted to one major question – the one about suffering. But then after that, people wanted to go on meeting! After nine sessions, those coming decided that they would quite like to do a course on basic Christian stuff. So we started with *Start!* (CPAS) – and now that we're coming up to Easter, and we've just about completed, we've got to ask them, 'What next?'[13]

Travelling empty-handed in this way has three great assets. First, it impels the Christian community into massive dependence upon the activity and real presence of the Spirit of God to lead the mission. For the apostolic person, it means learning to draw on the immediate power and presence of the Spirit within, and, because of that, the Holy Spirit is free to engage in the dynamics of the missionary task. Then it means that there is likely to be a true meeting between both parties, an exchange – which may also mean that the 'transaction', if there is one, is likely to be more appropriate to the requirement, to fit the bill. It's no good saying religious words to a man whose immediate need is a warm coat (see James 2.14-17). And, thirdly, it tends to turn the task of mission into an adventure. It is much more fluid, more interesting, more creative and more satisfying than simply delivering parcels!

6 Two by two

'The Lord . . . sent them two by two.'

Luke 10.1

Confidence in community

Even with all its attendant weakness and sinfulness, when lived well in the power of the Spirit Christian community is testimony. It points towards the kingdom of which it is a sign – in fact, not simply a sign, but *the* sign. There is great power in this, not the power to dominate, but the power to transform. It is not just a sign to look at, but also a sign to live in and under. People can get healed through being accepted in the community of Christ. Local communities can be changed through the activity of the local church.

It is perhaps time for the Church to remind itself that what the Church is, when it is being what it should be, has the power to heal: that 'good' community is itself an agent of healing and change. It is time, because there is at present a great deal of concern and anxiety about how to reach a postmodern culture for Christ. While this concern is legitimate, the anxiety is regrettable. The anxiety, in part, seems to be rooted in a crisis of confidence in our ability to communicate with such a culture. 'Postmodernism' seems like a Goliath before which the average church community quakes. 'How can we possibly meet this challenge? How can we ever hope to cross the great cultural divide that has opened up between the church and our culture?' But postmodern people have one huge factor in common with us. They are made of flesh and blood. They laugh. They cry. They sweat. They get puffed when they run for the bus. Their hearts beat faster when they are afraid. They like to be liked. When they feel peckish, they'll open the door of the fridge and have a little snack. They are glad when Friday comes.

Bridging the gap

The bridge that connects the Church to postmodern people is the same bridge that Jesus used when going to his culture. It is the bridge of our humanity. And our humanity lived out in community is just about the most powerful and compelling thing in the world. We need to be confident in this: it really is true, and it really works – our humanity connects us to others. As Christian people, the more authentic our humanity, the more at ease we are with ourselves and the more the Christian community becomes the locus for that humanity, then the more compelling our testimony.

Of course, as *Mission-shaped Church* reminds us, we need to 'go' in mission and search for places where we can connect our humanity to that of those to whom we are sent. Those early missionaries were encouraged by Jesus to connect to the person of peace, to lock their small communities of two on to other communities so that there could be some 'flow'. We can go in the confidence that although we may be small in the face of Goliath, what we have is *good*, what we have is *wanted*, what we have is *being sought*. Do we believe this?

Two by two: small but effective

'Two by two' *is* small. Some of the towns and villages into which those first missionaries were sent had sizeable populations. And those who carried the message of the kingdom were by no means experts in mission. But small can still be effective. And our humanity is a bridge strong enough to carry the gospel message.

I moved to Doncaster in 2002, and wanting to get to know the place to which I had come, I asked a friend to show me round the town, including the red-light district. I walked around that night in the pouring rain wondering whether there was something I could do to bring the gospel to the young girls on the streets. I decided to do some research – were any other Christians involved already? This threw up some interesting facts. One was that most of the girls were underage. Secondly, they were almost all addicted to the heroin that was part of the cycle of abuse set up by the pimps. And, thirdly, yes – there was a small but growing work among the prostitutes. Its story is simple but telling.

With two flasks of coffee

Two middle-aged women, worshippers at the Pentecostal church in the town centre, and in the heart of the red-light district, said to each other one day, 'What can we do? Many of these girls are children. We can't go on walking past them to church and look our Father God in the face in worship. But what can we do? We know nothing about drugs. We know nothing about prostitution. What are we to do?'

So, they did what they could. They made up two flasks of hot coffee and began taking it out to the girls on the streets. 'You look cold out here, and we've brought you a drink.' That's how they started. Since then, the work has grown. There is now a drop-in place for the prostitutes where they can get health-care advice, and support if they want to come off 'the game'. And some of the young women have come to faith. It all started with a compassionate 'seeing' and with a micro-mission, two by two, with two flasks of coffee and a lot of warm human love.[1]

Going 'two by two' into mission means that something bigger than the sum of the two (or more) people is on offer. The gospel invitation is to *participate in* something (the life of the Trinity itself) rather than to subscribe to a particular set of doctrinal tenets. Going two by two acts as a carrier, therefore, for the divine life into which people are invited to enter. It is clear that one of the overriding convictions of the movement associated with *Mission-shaped Church* is that mission is essentially relational.

> The gospel is the gracious intrusion of the precious gift of divine community into human experience . . . no wonder that in the New Testament the missionary enterprise was almost always carried forward by *teams*.[2]

There is a glorious, active buoyancy about a community charged with the energy of the Spirit, and this active buoyancy provides a compelling context for the true hearing of the gospel. For the gospel of acceptance can be truly heard when it is enfleshed in a body of people who are beginning to learn how to accept and welcome each other, warts and all. The gospel of forgiveness can be truly heard when it is understood in a group of people who are learning to forgive. The good news that I can 'be myself' can be most particularly heard when I meet a group of people who are learning how to live without masks. And the disturbing ethics of the kingdom can only be begun to be practised, it can only be done, when done together.

Quality matters

What, then, are some of the issues of which a church leadership should be aware as it considers its common life in relation to mission? Clearly, the importance of the *quality* of that common life cannot be overstated if 'the basic building block of the local church . . . should be the small group of Christian people who together form a transforming community'.[3]

The authors of *Mission-shaped Church* highlight the importance of small groups, both for discipleship and for relational mission, as one of the common features of most, if not all, fresh expressions. They write:

> The mission style of café churches is relational. It narrows the gap between what is encountered in an Alpha course and what is often negatively experienced on a Sunday. In Alpha people sit around in groups, and a sense of participation and response is more easily achieved.[4]

The conviction is, then, that the primary way forward in mission in our context is to do with relationships. If this is true, then high on the list of priorities for those who have apostolic intent must be the need to give attention to the quality of our common life in its many local expressions (both traditional and new).

Recognizing the Net

One of the most powerful and consistent images of evangelism in the New Testament is that of fishing: 'Follow me, and I will make you fishers of men – and of women and children.' And one of the most effective nets by which people can find ourselves lovingly 'caught by God' is the Net that is constituted by the network of loving, committed relationships in the Christian community, especially when that community defines its boundaries by what is called 'the centred set'.[5] This term describes a church in which those in the core community, rather than requiring commitment to a doctrinal position before accepting someone, recognize the direction in which that person is facing, and accept them because they are 'moving towards the centre'. The invitation to 'belong' before 'believing' is, in fact, the invitation to come and discover the truth of the gospel by living in the company of those who believe it. In an age of hi-tech isolationism we need, surely, to recognize and to celebrate the power of 'the Net', the healing potential of human relationships in the Body of Christ.

Dave and Heather Male are leaders of a Christian community in Huddersfield that is actually called 'The Net'. The church's mission statement reveals a primary concern with relationships: 'By knowing and loving God and each other we seek to enable non-churched people to develop a real and relevant relationship with Jesus.' One of their members has said, 'The church is built on relationships; it is a church of hope, a church of people.'

The Net

story story story story

Debbie and Jeff, members of The Net in Huddersfield, invited their neighbour, Angela, who is a college lecturer in nursing, to a carol service at a local hotel.

Angela said: 'It was funny, they used media clips, it made me laugh.' She attended a few of the University Hall meetings and found them non-threatening: 'I didn't feel judged, or pressurized or that the person at the front was controlling.'

She signed up for a 'Just Looking' course: 'It was eight weeks looking at faith in depth and I met others like me.' She was impressed that church people she didn't know invited her and her husband to lunch. Robin Gamble (a visiting evangelist) came to preach and invited those who felt they believed in Jesus to stand. She felt herself hovering on the chair, but unable to stand. The next week, she asked if she could say

> something at the end of the service. She said, 'I want to be
> one of you. This is the path I have chosen.' It was a relief and
> the climax of a dawning.
>
> Her declaration prompted three others to become Christians
> after the service. The bubble with which Angela tells her story
> is accompanied by admission of a long road. 'With hindsight I
> had been looking for a long time.'[6]

'I want to be one of you. This is the path I have chosen.' Here's someone
meeting the Christian community, clearly liking what she sees, and
recognizing that they are a community going somewhere together, a
community 'on the way'. It is significant that Angela's way of converting was
to say she wanted to belong to the group, 'to be one of you'. She was
joining up, becoming part of a movement.

Travelling in

But if seekers are going to be able to join up, to become part of a
movement, they have to be able to get close to those who are more
towards the centre. And over and over again, one of the problems that
people find when they come into the church community is that they are 'on
the outside' of the significant groups or relationships that are operating in
the church. They are kept at arm's length. They are greeted at coffee time,
but when they offer to help in the kitchen, or with putting away chairs, the
response is in the negative. As they walk home after two years of attending
church they may find themselves reflecting that they still don't really know
anyone: that there seems to be an 'in group', that they are definitely not part
of what is 'really going on in the church'.

If we want a community to be truly apostolic, we need to be assisting
people to travel much more freely from the edge towards the centre.
'Welcome' is not just what happens on the door; it is the whole process by
which someone moves from the periphery of a church community towards
the core. Many churches that pride themselves on being friendly are in fact
only friendly to those on the inside. And while many in our congregations

have hearts that are wide open to the stranger, there can be other, more covert, doorkeepers – the ones who really decide who gets to stay, who is accepted. As one clergyman said to me wearily, 'I get them in but I have a churchwarden who is determined to get them out again.'

How we can assist 'travelling in'

It can be the simplest thing that begins to help people to 'come in':

- the kitchen team, at Sunday coffee, accepting the offer of help from the widow, who's just started coming to church, with an, 'Oh, great – could you give us a hand?';

- the maintenance team inviting 'fringe' people to come and help clear the churchyard of litter and brambles and to have fish and chips afterwards;

- an invitation to Alpha, Emmaus, *Start!* . . . or another relationally based course, which includes an opportunity to eat a meal together.

Beverley's story

Beverley had a baby and she brought him for baptism. She joined the church mums' and toddlers' group and enjoyed helping out when needed in the kitchen. She began to take an active role in the leadership of the group and found herself developing deep friendships with the other leaders. She became interested in another church group that met to worship through the use of dance and she was invited to come along. She enjoyed the friendships and honesty within the group, as well as the creativity. It all began to fall into place: she began to feel she belonged, she liked being with these people, and she connected with using the body in worship. After some time, she was asked if she would like to attend a nurture course and through that she made a commitment to Christ.

Relational evangelism is, at heart, simple. Like 'two by two', it is not dependent on sophisticated techniques, or massive material resources. Most people can make relationships, especially where there is an atmosphere of trust. Children can. Grandparents can. Single mums can. Young men can. Successful middle-aged couples can. It shouldn't perhaps surprise us that we've been given something that we *can* do! But it does. In our rush to embrace models of evangelism that are mass-produced, we have often succeeded in removing evangelism from the sphere of human relationships and thus from the capabilities of most of the people in our churches. Making community together is not rocket science. But has it, perhaps, been convenient to us in the churches of the West to think that evangelism is something for the experts? It may be easier to run around looking for alternative solutions than face the simple one that is before us.

For although relational evangelism is not difficult – it *is* costly. It means giving ourselves to others. Perhaps to many others. It means letting them into my life, not just nodding at them with a smile on Sundays. It remains true that if I want to see life, I must give my life. If I want to see love, I must give love. And that self-giving has to be happening at the centre of the common life. The church's leadership has to take the lead.

Leadership with *koinonia* at the core

The quality of a Christian community is highly dependent upon the quality, not of the gifts, but of the relationships that are operating at the leadership level. A church (whether traditional or fresh expression) that is discovering a strong common life is therefore very likely to be one in which relationships between those in leadership roles are marked by commitment, trust and reality. The common life may begin with just two people, but it sets the tone for the whole community and engenders similar qualities – a family likeness – throughout the church. A staff team, a leadership team, a pastoral team that begins to try to live out the values of community will discover that the power of that common life ripples out into the whole church. If there is confidentiality, respect and commitment at the centre, similar values, and ways of relating, are much more likely to grow in the community as a whole.

For the ordained leader, this means, above all, being willing to become vulnerable, to own personal weakness, to take off the mask that the office can impose and to become a real person to those with whom life is to be shared. This is likely to be, as it seemed to be with Jesus, not a blanket vulnerability to all, but degrees of openness with different groups and teams. It would seem that Jesus himself found different ways of sharing life – with the twelve, with the three, and with the family at Bethany. It is interesting to reflect that he was clearly willing to let some of those people into the knowledge of his own particular temptations – those things in him on which the whole mission could have shipwrecked. How many clergy can, or would, do *that* with their staff teams?

A doorway to community

George Lings, of the Sheffield Centre, researching 'cell church' believes that without honesty it is impossible to enter cell life:

Through the visit to Totton an intriguing suspicion arose. It began with the cell leaders who kindly gave up an evening to meet me, to give their take on the evolving story and respond to the inevitable barrage of questions put. At one point, I posed the open question, 'What are the values of cell and which have you found has been most important?' I expected, because of their background of doing cell by the book, that 'Jesus at the centre' would be reiterated in some way. I was intrigued that the honest answer was 'honesty' – the last named value. Yet careful reading of the values might have told me that. The honesty value is described as a doorway to community.[7]

Without honesty there cannot be community. And good community means that there is a place safe enough for honesty to grow, so that the common life deepens. Many people are longing to find a safe place where they can be themselves. Will they find it among God's people? Are we a safe place? Are we learning, as a leadership team, to be ourselves with each other?

Attending to the Net

A church that is developing a truly apostolic spirituality will be a church, then, that sets a high value on maintaining the quality of its internal relationships. It is inevitable that in the rough and tumble of life the Net will become damaged. There will be tears in the fabric, and there will be holes, sometimes large, gaping ones, so that the Net is almost incapable of holding the fish that are there, never mind catching any more. Not only that, but the healing of the sick, the making people whole, that is such an important part of the apostolic mandate, is best done in the context of a community that is itself being made whole.

This means that giving attention to the Net is an important part of apostolic life, and that setting up structures to provide for such attention is time well spent. Structures will vary but they may include:

● building and developing a strong pastoral team;

● regular teaching on relationships and the practice of forgiveness;

● agreeing about the rules of confidentiality and holding to them;

● investing time in social events, especially in sharing meals;

● developing the church's ministry in the area of emotional healing and/or counselling skills.

As the church moves into mission, two things are very clear. One is that, increasingly, people are coming to faith out of dark and turbulent personal histories. The other is that the church needs to be ready to receive them with a love that is strong enough to bear with them as they journey towards transformation. And the church needs to be wise enough to practise careful 'damage limitation' on the destruction that such hurting people can inflict on a community in which they are meeting love, perhaps for the first time. For when frozen people begin to thaw in the warmth of God's love, the pain of remembered hurt can be excruciating. The best and safest place for this to happen is with a group of people who will not be afraid of the darkness because they are learning how to meet and face their own. So how are we getting on with facing our own darkness? How far on are we in our own journey of emotional intelligence? What can help us move on a bit? These might be important questions for church leaders to keep in mind for their Christian communities on the journey ahead.

An earthed spirituality

At its heart, then, apostolic spirituality will always be a communal spirituality. Perhaps that is because the sending God is himself not a lonely monad but communal in essence. There are many indications that the rediscovery of community will be the key to mission for the foreseeable future. This is going to be hard work. Apostolic spirituality is an earthed spirituality, and its ground is community. That may mean that, like learning to take nothing, there's a long journey to take. Parish churches, café churches, cathedrals, cell churches, schools' churches, youth congregations – some of us may have a lot of relearning to do in the journey to community. Building community is actually about sharing life, and sharing life is essentially practical. It bends the sinews as well as the mind. It asks as much of the flesh as of the spirit. It means loving in deed as well as in word. But if we can do it, if we can live it, it will be healing for the Church and bread for the world.

7 Prayer, promise and struggle

'So I say to you: Ask and it will be given to you.'

Luke 11.9

Prayer on Toast

There was a small group of young people attached to Holy Trinity Coventry when the then youth worker, Mark Tanner,[1] challenged them to pray. The challenge was this: As you've got to change buses in the centre of town for the school bus, and the bus stop is outside the church – how about coming an hour earlier – you pray – we'll make breakfast for you! That's how *Prayer on Toast* began. Soon the small group grew to 25: three years later there were 40 young people praying specifically for other young people and for mission among their peers.

Was it 'just coincidence', then, that when the church began to explore a venue for a youth event in the city centre, the manager of one of the night clubs, *The Dog and Trumpet*, offered his club free to them one Monday night a month, complete with non-alcoholic bar and bouncers? Or that a Youth For Christ mega-mission to the city resulted in over 300 new commitments and recommitments?

Prayer is the crunch issue for mission. It is the one vital ingredient. Those who set out on the journey of mission cannot do so without prayer because the journey cannot be undertaken without the Holy Spirit, and the way to access the Spirit and the Spirit's power is through prayer. 'Stay in the city', urged Jesus, 'until you have been clothed with power from on high' (Luke 24.49).

But the prayer isn't only to start us off. Mission very often leads us into the broken places of the world. It means engaging with complex situations, with subtle and demanding relationships. It means being close to hurting people and communities. It is more than getting what we need from God, important as that is. It's actually about doing mission *on a different level*. So in this chapter I want to explore three aspects of prayer. The first is the 'dynamic of dependence' that is at the heart of prayer. The second is how this dependence can open the door for the joy, vitality and life that is the Spirit's gift to the people of God, and without which the apostolic mission cannot take place. And the third is how prayer can be about doing mission on a different level.

Turning to God

There are, of course, as many different ways of praying as there are people, rhythms, seasons, times, places and opportunities – personal and corporate, silent and verbal, sung and spoken, liturgical and extempore, mental and bodily. There are prayers of confession, of adoration and contemplation, of thanksgiving, of petition and of intercession. There are prayers that wrestle with 'the powers', prayers of joy and prayers of pain. But the *movement* of prayer (which includes acts of liturgical worship) remains the same – it is a kind of 'turning towards God', almost (if you want) a kind of conversion, a re-turn, a reorientation of the human person, or persons, towards the one we know as the Father of Jesus Christ. And those who are advanced in prayer and in years – and they very often go together – will tell us that this 'turning' can become a constant, internal habit whereby the doorway between the self and God the Father is standing open more or less all the time.

The dynamic of dependence

When we try to unpack and understand what is going on in this movement towards God, we can perhaps see that underneath it all is the acknowledgement (whether realized or not) of *dependence*. Dependence is a word with a poor press in Western culture, associated as it is with felt weakness, with 'lack', with incompleteness: it is an offence to the dominant values of affluent humanism. It is true, of course, that 'dependence' needs to be an appropriate dependence, and that wrongful dependence leads to gross immaturity and much social ill. Yet as we become slowly and painfully aware of our deep dependence upon the ecological balance of the earth, and of the interdependence of all living organisms, we are perhaps discovering what a healthy kind of dependence might look like – something akin to humility, something that acknowledges that the human ego is not the rightful centre of all that is.

Prayer starts here. It is ultimately based on the recognition that to choose to be alone is to be less than human, that to be human we need to know our need of God. Indeed, when we know this, we can be called 'blessed' (Matthew 5.3). This dependence is not 'something we grow out of', some unfortunate weakness that came with Adam's downfall and departs with the second Adam. Jesus himself knew that he could do nothing by himself but could do only what he saw his Father doing (John 5.19). Seemingly, living in dependence is the conduit for that wholeness that is the goal of the kingdom – 'that all of them may be one, Father, just as you are in me and I am in you' (John 17.21). But it's not just one way, either. There are some good reasons for believing that God has made himself pretty dependent on us, too.

Nowhere does this dependence become more marked than in mission. Apostolic people are those who, in the words of a monk in Patmos, 'lean on Jesus' breast and feel the heartbeat of God'.[2] They are those who, when faced with the world's hungers, are encouraged to know themselves to be empty and so turn persistently to the Father (Luke 11.5-8).

Apostolic people are forcibly reminded again and again of how very great is their need for dependence upon the Holy Spirit. As one young person engaged in mission in Sheffield has expressed it, 'There has had to be a massive increase in the time I spend with God! I need him so much more. I want to be "in tune" with him all the time, to hear what I should be doing each day/who I should be seeing.'[3] While another wrote almost ruefully, 'It's frustrating to know that friendship evangelism is nothing without the back-up of a deep prayer life.'[4]

Led into the wilderness

It is perhaps not by coincidence, therefore, that one of the marks of apostolic people is likely to be that they frequently experience life as though they were in some kind of wilderness. It may be the wilderness of testing and temptation, the wilderness of dereliction, of emptiness, the wilderness of loneliness, in which the barren landscape of the inner life is exposed and experienced, the wilderness of bereavement, or of long passages of physical or emotional pain. These dark passages of the human spirit are often holy ground and one treads around them carefully when writing about them. Suffering of any kind is a mystery and mystery's depths can't be plumbed. Yet it's probably true that nowhere are the lessons of dependence learned more effectively than through the very hard experiences of felt emptiness, of bankruptcy, of brokenness, of weakness. It is in the wilderness that we learn how to lean.

Tell them yourselves

The small church in an urban priority area in the north decided to have a mini-mission. Because of its smallness it decided that it would be a good idea to invite a team from a big, 'successful' church. Much prayer and excitement went into the preparations. About ninety guests came to a pie and pea supper and then to a 'presentation' in the church. It was then that the evening began to nosedive. The visiting team failed to connect with the locals. People – many of them men – were getting up and walking out. Some were angry about being 'talked down to'.

The church members were distraught. It had taken years of careful pastoral care to develop the relationships with those people. Then God spoke to them, through one of their number. 'If you want them to know me, you have to tell them yourselves.' Out of the dereliction of apparent failure a new understanding of their call emerged. The church began to look at other ways of getting people interested, ways that were appropriate for the people in their area: pub nights, a second-hand clothes and furniture shop, sport. And it began to have an effect. The place of dereliction became the place of deeper dependence on God. Through that painful experience, the missionary call, and the imagination to fulfil it, was printed indelibly onto the heart of the church.[5]

Most of us will recognize the cycle of being led into the wilderness and coming up from it, 'leaning upon the beloved' (Song of Songs 8.5, NRSV), and know it to be all part of the genuine apostolic life. There is no other real way to be prepared for mission. That is not to deny the importance of lessons in cross-cultural communication, in language, in the prevailing philosophies and thought-forms and habits and cultures of those to whom we are sent. But the deepest preparation for individuals, and for churches, is in the heart, where the lessons learned are imparted to, branded on to, the individual or collective psyche.

Not to demoralize but to equip

If the wilderness were the last word, it would be deeply depressing and demoralizing. But it's not. The very ambiguity of the wilderness experience for Jesus – 'led by the Spirit to be tempted by the devil' – suggests that, in spite of the darkness and the alienation of the desert place, the Spirit of God is involved, and is, in fact, to be seen as the initiator. For, ultimately, the wilderness serves to remind us that we are empty. Its purpose is not to demoralize us but to equip us. Luke tells us, 'Jesus, full of the Holy Spirit . . . was led by the Spirit in the desert, where for forty days he was tempted by the devil' but then goes on to say that he returns from the desert *'in the power of '* the Spirit (Luke 4.1, 14). Is Luke just trying to find another way of saying the same thing? Or is he suggesting that something happened to Jesus in the desert place – something transformative, something that has had a marked effect upon him so that he is now equipped for what lies ahead?

When we reflect on these two closely linked experiences – the baptism in which Jesus knows who he is and that he is deeply loved, and the wilderness in which he discovers that, even though he is loved, the mission can nevertheless shipwreck because of his own inherent weakness – we can possibly imagine how the wilderness plunges him into an ever-deeper dependence upon God. We can see how it might be that through this dependence, this leaning hard, the ministry that he exercises is empowered, not by his own ego, but by the Spirit of God. For it is on his return from the desert 'in the power of the Spirit', that Jesus begins to preach and to heal and 'news about him spread through the whole countryside' (Luke 4.14).

The promise of the Spirit

The wilderness serves not to demoralize us, but to equip us. That is good news for churches as well as individuals. The wilderness is not the last word because the last word belongs to the Spirit: 'Wait for the gift my Father promised, which you have heard me speak about . . . in a few days you will be baptised with the Holy Spirit . . . you will receive power when the Holy Spirit comes on you; and you will be my witnesses in Jerusalem, and in all Judea and Samaria, and to the ends of the earth' (Acts 1.4, 5, 8). When the Spirit does come, the joy, vitality and life that are his gift are massively attractive. After Pentecost, those first disciples find that they cannot help but speak about what they have seen and heard. They also discover that although they are quite ordinary 'unlettered' people, they are able to communicate across massive cultural and linguistic divides. They begin to share a common life, which touches their wallets as well as their worship. Like lightning finding its way to earth, the Spirit earths himself in the human community – and the effects are life changing.

'Lord, turn me round'

The vicar leaned up against the side of the kitchen units in the vicarage. She was filled with a great weariness. 'There must be a better way of doing it all than *this*,' she thought to herself. Shortly after, she had a dream in which she could see that she was heading in the wrong direction. On awaking, she began to pray earnestly, 'Lord, turn me round.' It was a prayer that was to engage her for the next four years. 'Lord, turn me round. I'm going in the wrong direction. Turn me round.' She prayed at the bus stop. She prayed in the car. She prayed while walking the dog. 'Lord, turn me round.' During those four years, she felt, if anything, even more bankrupt. But she also began to see that some of the things that were driving her in ministry were more to do with personal ambition than with the Holy Spirit. She was a 'signed-up' charismatic, but she was still operating largely out of her own ego. No wonder the ministry was exhausting. She argued a lot with God in that period. She could see clearly that to be fully identified with what is often perceived as 'the foolishness' of the Spirit would have implications. But she was desperate and in the end she gave in. She said, 'Yes' to God, whatever it might mean.

And what happened next was utterly life changing. She made a trip to a well-known centre of renewal in Canada. She was there a week and during that time it seemed that God took her apart and put her together again. All the pain and the exhaustion and the anxiety and the fears were washed away in a flood of the Spirit's presence. She was filled with the Holy Spirit in a new way. From then on, her life took on a different shape and her ministry changed radically. Even though she continued to work hard, there was an 'ease' about it — ministry became fun. And she became much more intentional about mission.[6]

But in this description of the Spirit's coming, are we not in danger of a kind of easy triumphalism? Are we deceiving ourselves? Are we massively repressing 'the dark side': possibly doing a cover-up job? A glimpse at the subsequent lives of those caught up in that first wave of the Spirit's coming might provide us with something of a reply to this legitimate question. For, plunged into mission in the power of the Spirit, they found that in their normal lives they were frequently 'hard pressed on every side, but not crushed; perplexed, but not in despair; persecuted, but not abandoned; struck down, but not destroyed' (2 Corinthians 4.8-9). They discovered the shape and meaning of apostolic life to be cross-shaped. The Spirit and the cross can never be divided — and those who share in the power of the Resurrection must also share in our Lord's sufferings (Philippians 3.10).

If felt weakness is a precondition for the Spirit's power, then it can be argued that the churches in England today find themselves in the best possible place to begin to wait again, in a new and deeper way, for the Spirit's coming. It may be that as a local church community we are at present feeling particularly weak and vulnerable. We don't quite know what is going on. But perhaps God himself has led us to this place? Perhaps some of the feelings of helplessness and dismay at our own lack can lead us into a deeper dependence upon God and consequently the possibility of a greater empowerment for mission through the Holy Spirit? If this is the case, how can we assist in this process? How do we receive the Spirit?

Ask, seek, knock

The problem with posing the question, 'How do we receive the Spirit?' is that we run the risk of trying to find a formula, whereas we know that there is no formula and that the Spirit moves where he wills. But there are *patterns* that can provide pointers, nudges, clues. One of these is the pattern of spiritual renewal that we have already outlined – emptiness, brokenness, wilderness, leading to an awareness of lack, of need, of hunger, and a consequent turning, or re-turning, to God. When that happens, another pattern emerges – that of persistent waiting, asking, seeking, knocking. A certain engagement is required of us. This asking, seeking, knocking may, of course, take some time. It will assume different shapes for different people and different traditions and churches. But the promise is that to those who ask, it will be given; those who seek, find; to those who knock, the door will be opened (Luke 11.9-10). It's vital to note that these well-known words are actually spoken in reference to the giving of the Holy Spirit. And that the whole is in the context of teaching on prayer, and on dependence upon God for the supply of resources for the task ahead. What's more, the fruit of 'ask-seek-knock' is hammered home in a six-fold repetition: 'It will happen, it will happen, it will happen, it will happen, it will happen, it will happen.'

If we want to change the imagery, John gives us another picture (John 7.37), but the pattern is the same: thirst, come, drink. And the outcome is the same: an outflow of the Spirit's life, water for a thirsty world.

Asking for the Spirit is, in fact, the simplest thing in the world. Not *easy*, because, as we have seen, it may mean that to get to the place of asking, we are led through a wilderness. But simple in the sense that it requires childlikeness, and the final acknowledgement that without God we can be and do nothing. There can be no truly apostolic spirituality without an experience of the Holy Spirit, present, living and active among us, for the Spirit is himself *apostolic* – the one who is sent. And asking for the Spirit may mean taking a risk. For who knows what will happen when God sends the Holy Spirit? Is he safe? Or, to put it another way, no – he's not safe. But he is *good*.[7]

Asking and expectancy

The act of asking suggests that we know that there is *something to be received*. When we see that the wilderness leads us to felt dependence, when we dare to believe that the experience of bankruptcy or emptiness is not to demoralize us but to equip us, when we take seriously the words spoken to us – that the Father wants to send us the Spirit – then we begin to ask expectantly. Expectant waiting means that we wait with anticipation rather than with an agenda. The element of surprise is part of the Spirit's gift. All we need to know is that we need God, and we need him more than ever before if we are to do the kind of mission to our culture that is being required of us. This expectant waiting is what constitutes faith: believing that what we ask for we will receive. Are we ready to stick our necks out and believe it?

Receiving the Spirit

In spite of the danger of reducing the mystery of the Spirit's coming to a formula, many people throughout the Church's long history and various traditions would say that there is a definite 'before and after' to receiving the Holy Spirit. That doesn't mean that there is necessarily an overwhelming experience of receiving him – though that is not unusual. What it means is that when the Spirit comes, we begin to experience the effect (what the Bible calls 'fruit') in our lives. This can be as true for those of us who have been faithful churchgoers all our lives as it is for returning prodigals.

Because of this 'before and after', sometimes a formal prayer for the coming of the Spirit can be significant. Not always and not in every case: we must again stress that there is no formula for this. The Spirit can come to us through faithful feasting on the sacrament – St Ephraim the Syrian wrote, 'He who eats this bread with faith eats at the same time the fire of the Holy Spirit.' The Spirit can come through feasting upon the word of God. But for some people and for some church communities, a 'formal act' of asking, and of believing that as-we-ask-so-we-receive can be an important marker.

If we believe (as a decision to dare to trust God) that we receive when we ask, then the encouragement to give thanks in faith will be an important constituent in this action. Mary burst out into a song of thanksgiving and praise on the basis of the angel's promise, before she experienced the tangible reality of what was promised. Thanksgiving is the activity of faith. For those who, in the past, have asked for the Spirit and, frankly, have been disappointed that 'nothing seems to happen', this question of thanksgiving, the thanksgiving that is faith in action, can be the key they need. A simple prayer of asking, a subsequent act of thanksgiving that as God promises, so God gives, and then the decision to live believing that the Spirit has come and that we will see the fruit in our lives and experience, may be all that is needful.

Saturated with God

But can we imply that faithful churchgoers may need to be filled with the Spirit? Do not all Christians have the Spirit of Christ? Well, yes and no! Of course, we cannot be Christians without the indwelling presence of the Christ. But what can only be described as the *fullness* of the Spirit – the overflow of power and love and joy and peace, the sense of being saturated with God (like a chamois leather that has been dried up and is dropped into a bucket of water), our churches responsive to his leading and guiding into mission – can we be honest enough to confess that this we know we lack? Are we really sure we do not need 'something more' from God in order to fulfil the apostolic mandate? No wonder Paul, when urging the Ephesian Christians to be filled with the Spirit, uses the present continuous tense – literally '*go on being filled*' (cf. Ephesians 5.18). Complacency is a killer.

Enjoyment, delight and pleasure

In talking about the fullness of the Spirit, I am not arguing that all should become 'charismatics' in the sense of embracing the particular tradition that has become known as the charismatic movement. But I am convinced that we should all become charismatics in the sense of having a healthy, robust and living experience of the power and presence of the Spirit of God in our ordinary, everyday lives and in the ordinary, everyday lives of our churches. I would argue, in the strongest possible terms, that this is what God has intended by the giving of the Spirit – that the enjoyment, delight and pleasure in knowing him intimately through the Spirit's gift is the inheritance of all his children. This is the gospel – the good news that we are to take to all the world. How can we give away what we have not received ourselves?

Doing mission on another level

The prayer that is rooted in dependence is not only for us, but also for the world. And as we begin to move out into that world, intercession frequently cranks up several notches in our pattern of prayer. We start taking other people into God's presence, as this young man working in mission on the streets with the Jesus Fellowship discovered:

> Instead of being a trip off with God to some mystic plane (that is still a part every now and then, but that's no longer my definition of a 'good time of prayer'), prayer has become a constant 24/7 thing – and the faces of people or their needs come before me, constantly.[8]

When we start to truly 'see', or to contemplate, often the first and natural response is intercession. This is where the background work of mission is done. And work it can be, some of the hardest, most demanding work there is. It can be quite different, at times, from what we call 'the intercessions' on Sunday. It can have much more of a dimension of what we might call 'struggle'. Perhaps that's because intercession and 'the cross' are very deeply connected – for the cross is a kind of intercession-in-action. Intercession has deep connections with theologies of liberation and of social action; it is about wrestling in the deep places of the world for the world's freedom.

Freedom fighters

Jane was working in the kitchen when the door opened and her husband, David, entered. She noticed he was pouring sweat. 'What *have* you been doing?' she asked. 'Praying for Ruth,' he replied simply. Ruth was a young girl who was undergoing a kidney transplant. The transplant was successful and Ruth lived.[9]

Prayer as combat, as struggle, can be seen throughout the ministry of Jesus – just think for a moment about the relationship between casting out demons and prayer in the account of the healing of the boy with the evil spirit (Mark 9.28, 29). And Paul asks for prayer that 'whenever I open my mouth, words may be given me so that I will fearlessly make known the mystery of the gospel' (Ephesians 6.19) – in the context of writing about struggling with principalities, with powers, and about the armour of God. The Desert Fathers and Mothers were noted for their 'battling with demons', a struggle that they knew to be a life-long commitment: 'With any other labour that a man undertakes in the life of religion . . . he has some rest; but prayer hath the travail of a mighty conflict to one's last breath.'[10]

This struggle, which is beyond our natural sight, is of cosmic proportions for those who pray. 'There really is a massive, albeit hidden struggle for the shape, governance and future of the world.' The writer, Walter Brueggemann, says that about what happens on the cross. He argues, in fact, that evangelism makes no sense unless the drama (of salvation) is understood agonistically – as having the character of struggle. Not everyone will agree with that understanding of salvation – but most people who get drawn into intercession will agree that it is massively demanding and can feel at times like wrestling with unseen forces. For although the ultimate victory for the world has been won on the cross, with the cross providing the 'decisive turn in our favour', the outworking is not yet fully realized. There is a job to be done. And it's a job shared with other Christians.

The Open Door church plant in Calne

Originally, we would just pray that the Lord would bring those he wanted, and that he would equip us to deal with whomever he sent: this prayer was generally confined to the Team. Now, after three years, we are moving towards more structured prayer for mission, and specific 'prayer gatherings' (small groups) meet to pray regularly for the 'outsiders' in our town. These come together periodically to share feedback and pray as a church . . . This has an interesting ecumenical dimension, since several denominations in Calne – traditional Anglican, Free, Catholic – seem to be called at the same time to mission, or at least, prayer for mission.[11]

There is a watch to be maintained. For a hundred years after the Great Awakening in 1727, Count Zinzendorf's Christian community maintained a round-the-clock prayer meeting for renewal and outreach. And, from a very different tradition, Thomas Merton writes of the place of the watcher – the one who waits and looks for the coming of the reign of God:

> We are exiles in the far end of solitude, living as listeners,
> With hearts attending to the skies we cannot understand,
> Waiting upon the first far drums of Christ the Conqueror,
> Planted like sentinels upon the world's frontier.[12]

Maintaining a watch is no easy task. Keeping attentive, keeping alert, keeping awake, and holding the world before God, silently or with words – this is the hidden work of the apostolic church. It's a way of doing mission on another level: holding the door open for God. At times it's a real struggle to keep that door open. Sometimes we will be aware of massive forces pushing against us, trying to get us to let go of that open door. It stretches us, and this is possibly why it can be, at times, also hugely exhilarating. So it's likely that an apostolic church, a church sent into the world, will be a church with its sleeves rolled up and ready when it comes to prayer. And that could be very good news for the Church.

8 The message and the messengers

'As you go, preach this message: "The kingdom of heaven is near."'

Matthew 10.7

Something happens to the friends of Jesus that makes them into messengers. Some great charge of energy transmits to them. They become utterly, radically different. The direction of their lives is changed. Their individual lives take on very different shapes from those that might have been expected. They discover themselves to be sent, *apostoloi*, to be bearers of a message, to be messengers. They are propelled into a massive adventure, which for many of them will end in their own suffering and deaths at the hands of those to whom they are sent.

Now we might think that dealing as they were with such massive themes, such a big news story, and finding it to be written increasingly in their own blood, those early messengers might have become more and more driven, more and more anxious, about the need to pass on their message. Yet nowhere is it recorded that they have to urge and exhort each other to engage in evangelism. Rather, it happens naturally and without inhibition. 'We cannot help speaking about what we have seen and heard,' say Peter and John, and Luke reports how they 'spoke the word of God boldly' (Acts 4.20,31). There was a kind of 'ease' about it all. That doesn't mean to say that they didn't speak thoughtfully – look at the way Paul carefully approached the culture of Athens. But it seems fairly clear that they reckoned they had good news to share and they wanted to pass it on. And from what we know of the first disciples, it wasn't that they had outstanding personal advantages. They were a very mixed bunch. Erratic in their loyalties, self-seeking at times, argumentative, theologically slow on the uptake, competitive – and 'unschooled, ordinary' people (Acts 4.13) to boot. Yet somehow they seemed compelled to spread the message. They were consumed with the message, they were convinced about the message – the message, and passing it on, had become the most important thing in the world. What was it?

We have already seen that the presence and power of the Spirit is an essential component of mission. But there is something else, something prior to the Spirit's coming. In fact, the Spirit cannot come to the Church without this prior event. It is event which is the kernel from which apostolic spirituality grows. It is the conviction that something never-seen-before has happened, that something has taken place that changes everything – about the world, about the way we understand it, about the future.

The heart of the gospel

At the heart of apostolic spirituality lies one great, central, bewildering, joyful, life-giving discovery – that Jesus is alive. Everything else really does flow from this. The significance of the Incarnation, the theology of the cross, the meaning of forgiveness, the overcoming of the old order, the birth of the new creation, the end of death and the beginning of the Church, the outpouring of the Holy Spirit – the elucidations and explanations of Christology and soteriology and ecclesiology – would have little meaning without this central fact that Jesus is alive. Even the claim that 'Jesus is Lord' (or, perhaps, to put it in a more postmodern way, 'Jesus is the Centre') finds its corroboration in the primary discovery that Jesus is alive. 'Jesus is alive – and, therefore, it is true – Jesus *really is* Lord.'

> Christianity is primarily news and only secondarily views.[1]

Branded with the message

This central conviction, that Jesus is alive, is woven into the heart and mind of the apostolic person: she is branded with it, marked with it; it is burned into the psyche. The message and the messenger become one. Sharing this conviction with others is not the primary thing, in spite of the paradoxical fact that sharing it frequently causes it to re-ignite in the messenger. First and foremost, the message informs and shapes the messenger. It is a message with massive impact upon the human person – and through the human person into human communities. It is entirely and utterly transformative and those who receive it have the chance to be never the same again.

Life-changing

She was a real, bitter, hard-faced person. No one in the community bothered much with her because she could be so difficult. She was very angry with the local church because of the loss of the traditional choir and changes that were happening. We (some of the church members) felt called to love her no matter what. This was not easy! We eventually invited her to do a Christian basics course at our house. She discovered that Jesus loved her. She was filled with such joy that her character completely changed. She was full of joy ... The change in her was a witness to those in church who had never seen the like, and to her family. Her husband started to attend. She died not long after, unexpectedly – and suddenly we were grief-stricken. Everybody had come to love her dearly. Her husband stayed at church – until he too went to be with the Lord.[2]

Deep wells, bubbling fountains

An apostolic community will be one that is branded with, burned with, the conviction that Jesus is alive. This conviction may be held deeply and quietly or it may bubble joyfully and exuberantly on the surface – but it must be there. The conviction does not exclude times of doubt and darkness, puzzles to solve and mysteries to ponder. We have already seen in Chapter 3 that the relationship with God is a 'real' relationship, subject to twists and turns and ups and downs. It is quite possible to hold to the conviction that he is alive, even to experience something of the reality of that, while at the same time being puzzled, or doubting, or confused, or angry about the way his relationship with us is being lived out at a particular time. We can be convinced of a person's reality while at times doubting their dealings with us. Too, it is a conviction with inner coherence, supra-rational rather than irrational. It lays claim to be rooted in an historical rather than a psychological event: an event that can be explored, explained, argued, analysed, debated and discussed because it is focused upon a real person who really existed at a given place and a given time.

It is the message 'Jesus is alive' that the messengers are to proclaim one way or another, in word and deed. That is not to say that the content of the message is to be reduced to the shorthand of those three words. Nor is it to say that the proclamation will necessarily start with the news about Jesus Christ: in fact, the occasions when that is possible will be rare. We usually have to start a lot farther back, as Laurence and Beth Keith, both young lay people, whose experience of 'how we went and had to let go' we looked at in Chapter 5, were to find when they started meeting with people who were de-churched, or post-Christian.

story
story
story
story

Our foundations were challenged

In one meeting we asked them to say what words or concepts they struggled with. We anticipated 'leadership' and 'vision' coming from a church with strong leadership. We didn't anticipate 'prayer', 'Jesus', 'community' . . . There were a lot of tears that day as people were able to express hurts in a safe environment, but it made us realise we had to start much farther back and build new, appropriate foundations if we were going to really engage with post-modern people.[3]

How faith is key in announcing the presence of the future

The 'proclamation' side of mission has frequently been seen as the task of the clergy, with 'proclamation' being understood as preaching, often in an expository style, on the how and why of God's saving love. This kind of preaching is important, essential even. But it's not the only way of proclaiming the good news.

For, fundamentally, *keryssein* (which is often translated as 'preach') means the *declaration* of an event, a declaration that is both in word and in sign. As such, the very act of announcing — in word or deed — has within it the power to make present the future. It can do this because it *draws on, utilizes*, faith. In fact, faith is the beginning, middle and end of the whole endeavour. It's by faith that we announce, herald, introduce, the reign of God into the 'now'. It's faith that makes the act of proclaiming an action of realized eschatology – an action that makes the future present. So the eucharistic prayer of the Church can be described as *kerygmatic*.

A discovery

A fascinating surprise within Seeker service philosophy is their experience (at The Carpenter's Arms Church, Deal) of Communion as a focus for evangelistic commitment. Monthly, an aspect of the gospel was taught and related to breaking bread and outpouring of wine. In receiving, the indwelling of Christ was also highlighted. Other groups like Alternative Worship and some strands of Church for Gen X report similar evangelistic energy in the Eucharist. Their conviction grew that Christ being lifted up did draw people to himself. In Alan's words, 'This has been one of the most significant aspects of evangelism in The Carpenter's Arms. It is not only that people hear the Gospel through Communion, but it is there and then that the response can be made.'[4]

Faith in the risen Jesus, joyful, confident and believing – even when life is tough, when we don't understand what God is doing with us, when we are full of uncertainty – this kind of faith, which is not dependent upon 'feelings', is a major feature of apostolic spirituality. We won't get very far on the apostolic journey without it. And, paradoxically, of course, it grows and develops as we journey. There is nothing like seeing other people coming to faith in the risen Lord for strengthening our own! Could it be that one reason why 'faith' has often seemed at a low ebb in the Church has to do with 'settlement'? And might it be that going in mission, going with the message, can cause the great, dormant reserves of faith, which at present are lying – often untapped, unused and unrecognized – deep in the heart of the Church, to surge to the surface?

Who are the proclaimers – and how do they do it?

Getting the message out of church to its true home on the streets, 'out there', is, then, the task of mission. How we do this, how we proclaim the kingdom, is the question that faces each individual Christian and each church.

A dinner party

Sue and Edwin live in a big stone house in the centre of Sheffield and every Thursday they give a dinner party. Two large tables are laid and the food is carefully prepared – organic meat, home-made bread, fresh vegetables, meltingly scrumptious desserts. To the dinner party come street people – young men who live in squats, people just out of prison, addicts, rough sleepers. Very often there will be twenty of them there, and they are greeted with love and with welcome. It feels like home, like family. Sue and Edwin and their helpers sit and eat with them. It's a time to catch up, to share news. And there are always seconds. After the meal, they often have a simple quiz. If you live in a squat, and you feel like a nobody and you get one of the quiz questions right and everyone says, 'Well done!' it makes you feel – well, nice about yourself.

One evening the Bishop came. In the course of the meal, he took hold of the bread and said in the sudden silence, 'It was on a Thursday night that Jesus had a meal with his friends – the night before he died. He took bread and gave thanks for it, he blessed and he passed it round to his friends, saying, "This is my body: do this to remember me."' He began to pass the bread around the table. Then he picked up the jug of blackcurrant cordial. He continued: 'Jesus said, "This is my blood. Drink this to remember that I died for you."' The cordial was poured, all drank. And as they ate and drank, several of those young men began to weep.

Announcing the kingdom in word and deed, proclaiming it through both spoken and enacted words, is the goal of the apostolic journey. There is a message to be given, and the messengers are to deliver it in ways that make sense to those to whom they are sent. The giving of the message includes the healing of bodies and minds and the restoration of life: it makes possible the return of the outcasts and it expels evil (Matthew 10.7,8). It has the power to transform not only individuals but also whole communities. Because of the nature of the message, its origins and its goals, there is a legitimate apostolic confidence attached to it and to those who proclaim it. But how can we speak with confidence in an age of such uncertainty?

A crisis of confidence

We have already noted in Chapter 1 that there are particular contemporary concerns about confidence in matters of faith – and we have suggested that there is often confusion in the public mind between confidence and extremism. If we really do believe that Jesus Christ is alive, and is at the Centre, in the way that the Early Church clearly did, how can we hold to this and proclaim it in a way that is sensitive to an age both wary and weary of truth claims? To reiterate the key question raised in Chapter 1: If there is a Christian confidence that can work for our age, how can the whole Church be infused with it, so that the apostolate of the laity, as well as that of the clergy, can be liberated to become an apostolic people? Questions such as these form an essential part of the exhilarating task of mission today. They are questions with which those moving out into fresh expressions of church are having to grapple. But these are also questions for the whole Church, for the adventure, the journey of discovery, is open to all. One way forward may be through a fresh discovery and appreciation of *testimony*.

Truth-bearing stories

If the gospel is truth-bearing (and, as Christians, we believe that it is) then that truth is carried primarily through the vehicle of personal testimony. The gospel is packaged in the stories of people who met with Jesus and whose lives were changed, reshaped according to another pattern. So we have not just the gospel according to Matthew, or Mark, or Luke, or John – but the gospel according to a tax man called Zacchaeus (Luke 19.1-10); the gospel according to two unnamed blind men (Matthew 9.27-31); the gospel according to a group of parents with small children (Mark 10.13-16); the gospel according to a widow and her son who lived in a town called Nain (Luke 7.11-15). There are literally hundreds of them. The stories, of course, have been gathered together and shaped to form one story, the story of the one they are all about. But they are basically stories about how that one person impacted the many.

Testimony in the culture

The stories don't end with the closing of the canon of Scripture. In a very real sense, the canon is still open. For there is an undeniable sense in which the 'gospel stories' are still being written today – in the experience of contemporary people whose lives are being marked and transformed by that same person. This is the gospel story, contemporary, and in our midst, of Jesus. Told in testimony, these stories have the power to impact at a level that is transformative rather than simply discursive or didactive.

Now our contemporary culture is massively open to 'testimony'. Watch any TV chat show and what you see is testimony – Billy Connolly on how he survived an abusive father, David Beckham on how he copes with marriage, fame and football. More significantly, we see 'unknown', ordinary people talking about how they deal with the whole gamut of life's experiences – drugs, school, moral failure, divorce, accident, abuse, trauma – testimony is in the culture. It is as though, with the breakdown of confidence in institutional authority, and fewer opportunities to learn through the passed-on wisdom of the family, people are turning to one another to learn how 'to do life'. This is facilitated by the provision through high-tech media systems – Internet blogging, TV, radio, mobile phones, video – of places where experiences may be shared. And personal stories about personal journeys are not the only events being handled by ordinary people. Graphic incidents from the bomb attacks in London on 7/7 and the failed attacks two weeks later were recorded on mobile phones and videos as people fled the scene. Everyone had their own viewpoint, their own story to tell, woven into the bigger story. As a leading professor of journalism was later ruefully to admit, 'Journalists have lost their role as writing the first rough draft of human history.'[5]

It works for me

Our age is an age wary of truth claims but wide open to testimony. 'It works for me' is a respectable and pragmatic test for life in our culture: including the testing of issues of spirituality. *Why* it works for me, and *how* it works for me – the science of the thing – are of secondary importance, in the same kind of relationship to the core story as the science of theology to the gospel stories. 'It works for me' is transformative rather than manipulative. It can be highly challenging, prophetic, disturbing, unsettling, provoking, joyful, energizing, freeing to the one who encounters this testimony, but only by virtue of the power of the story that is being lived.

'It works for me' isn't just a kind of spiritual consumerism. It can call into question prevailing philosophies and powers. Look at the confusion and fury unleashed through the story told by the man born blind. The man wasn't a particularly gifted or clever theologian. He made it clear that there were gaps in his knowledge: he didn't have it all sewn up. When asked for a theological comment on the one who had healed him, he simply said, 'Don't know whether he's a "sinner" or not. One thing I do know. I was blind but now I see' (John 9.24-34). This story, with the incontrovertible evidence that accompanied it, produced a huge reaction. It was one of the events that shook the structure of Pharisaism to its foundations.

The Church of God has as many of these stories as it has members. Some are very simple: 'I go to church: I find it helpful.' Others tell dramatically of lives changed from darkness to light. The stories of some people, like Peter, are of great moral failure and of restoration; those of others, like Zacchaeus, of being set free from addiction to money. Some of the most fruitful are 'about us' as a Church, not just 'about me'. The group stories have a particular power to enable others to join the story. All are at their most powerful and life bearing when they are told in the context of great suffering.

It is time for the stories to be told. They can be told with confidence because they are non-coercive and they have their own inner integrity. They are not the last word on the Christian message, but they will very often be the first.

9 Helping to heal the world's woe

'Heal the sick, raise the dead, cleanse those who have leprosy, drive out demons.'

Matthew 10.8

One woman's journey

On Monday 4 March 1985 my 14-year-old daughter was knocked down by a car and suffered a fractured skull.

A brain scan two days later showed extensive brain damage and that night, after coming home from the hospital, I went for a walk. I had to walk past where I knew the vicar of the local church lived, and I found myself wanting to go and talk to him, but something told me that he wouldn't want to know because I didn't go to church and it would be hypocritical going to see him now I was in trouble, so on I walked round on to the main road where the accident had happened. I wandered up and down wondering how life could go on so normally when my world had fallen apart. On the way back home I found myself turning into the vicar's drive and knocking on the door. He invited me in and said the church had been praying for Kerry because one of the first people on the scene of the accident was a nurse who belonged to their congregation. He didn't tell me at the time that she had gone straight round to his house, praying, despite the fact she thought that Kerry wouldn't make it to the hospital, because of her head injury.

Over the next five weeks of intensive care there were many ups and downs, but every time I had bad news, like being sent for time and time again because they thought she wouldn't make it through the night, that her brain had swollen so she needed an operation, that she would need a tracheotomy, I found myself praying and these things didn't happen. She had infection after infection and they tried to take her off the ventilator four times before they succeeded.

But two things happened during this time that I believe were words from God for me. First of all, at the end of week one, after we'd been called back to the hospital because they thought she wouldn't make it through the night, she stabilized and we went home. At home I asked God to take Kerry to be with him if she was going to be brain damaged in any way. I said, 'If she's still alive in the morning then I will believe you are going to give her back to me.'

Then on the Wednesday of the second week we'd just come home from the hospital, and I was sitting down with a cup of tea, I distinctly heard footsteps coming down the path, and the porch door opening. I glanced at the clock. It was 9 o'clock, the time Kerry was due home the night of the accident. I got up to open the front door and then reality kicked in and I realized it couldn't be Kerry as she was in hospital. I looked through the window and nobody was there. I went up to bed and slept through for the first time since the accident.

In the morning I just had a feeling of knowing I can't describe any other way. I just *knew* that Kerry was coming home and it was God's way of telling me. My mother arrived and looked at me saying, 'Are you all right?' I said, 'Yes, Kerry's coming home, you know,' and she replied, 'Yes, I know.' And as we talked we found that she too had woken with that knowledge that we didn't understand. From then on I stayed positive and believed, no matter what happened or what the doctors told me, even when a brain scan registered there was no normal brain activity, no higher intelligence and the doctors said that the movements she'd started to make with her left arm and leg were only reflex.

That Sunday, two weeks after the accident, I went to church for the first time to thank the people who had been praying for us. As I experienced the service I realized these people had something I wanted, they knew something I didn't know. But the most amazing part of this story centres around Easter.

Good Friday was on 5 April, five weeks after Kerry's accident. I was met by a doctor who told me they wanted to move Kerry to another hospital because she didn't need intensive care any more but long-term care. My answer was, 'Great, then we can start physiotherapy and other rehabilitation.' The doctor looked me straight in the eye and said, 'If Kerry gets another infection the best thing to do would be not to treat her.' In other words, let her die, she's not going to get any better. But again I couldn't believe that because I had my 'words' from God, this knowledge of Kerry coming home.

On Easter Sunday I went on the local hill for the sunrise service at 6.30 a.m. Coming back to the car I turned on the radio and Cliff Richard was singing, 'When I survey the wondrous cross'. As I got to the hospital the staff nurse met me and said that Kerry had been touching the top of her head, she could still only move her left arm and leg. I went over and Kerry's fringe was so long by now it was in her eyes. I said we needed to move it out of her eyes and she lifted her hand and pushed the fringe back. I said, 'Kerry, move the hair out of your eyes,' and she did it again. I still didn't believe it so I asked her again and again she did it. The nurse was standing behind me amazed. After that things moved so fast it was unbelievable ... no, it was God.

We were told by the specialists in physiotherapy, speech therapy, occupational therapy, etc. that it would take years for Kerry to relearn these skills if ever she did, but all I did was go back to the church and ask that they pray for each thing as it came up, especially for her to speak, because I knew I could cope with her in a wheelchair if I had to, as long as we could communicate. The church prayed on the Sunday and on the

Monday Kerry said, 'Home.' She wanted to come home. Within four weeks she was home, walking a few steps, talking more or less normally. The doctor couldn't believe her progress. There was no need for any of their services and he brought four other doctors in to see her. Kerry went back to school for the mornings in June and full time in September, three months after her accident. She was discharged from the hospital altogether in October.

Kerry and I were both confirmed in January 1986. She married the vicar's son in June 1989 and they have three children. My mother also came to faith and was a loyal member of the church until her death in June 1994.[1]

The announcement enacted

Evangelism and healing go hand in hand. Just as the spoken announcement is for the streets, so is the enacted one. It may be about a physical healing, such as Kerry's, that leads to faith. It may result in neighbours who have fallen out being restored to friendship. It may be about the church and the community deciding to 'green' a site for children to play in. It may involve the church in an issue of justice to do with the local factory and their workers. It will almost certainly mean the ministry of healing into damaged and pained emotions and will include prayer for the expulsion of the demonic, whether from structures or from people. It is impossible to separate the message from the ministry of healing. They are inextricably bound up. Sometimes the very act of proclamation can cause healing to spring up. The proclamation is rooted in the Resurrection, and the Resurrection has power, the power to generate life.

For a long period, 'settlement' has meant that the ministry of healing – and, in particular, that of prayer for healing – has at times appeared to be locked away in the church. Church people do it for and with church people. But healing doesn't belong in the Church, just as the message doesn't belong in the Church. Even though the message forms and shapes the Church, and births the Church, it belongs in the world. And because healing is part of the message, the enacted bit, healing belongs in the world, too. The big question for an apostolic people is: How are we going to get the healing out?

One of the answers, of course, is that apostolically minded people *have* been getting the healing out, very often through loving service, through caring practically for broken people and broken places. But it's often been the case that a kind of wedge has been driven in the minds of Christians between the social gospel and the spiritual gospel, with different traditions cornering different bits of the market. It is hard to see how such an un-unified approach can really bring the kind of healing we all need.

For all healing, – ecological, communal, social, individual, emotional and physical – is an issue of spiritual healing, of restoration. We do not have a social gospel and a spiritual gospel, with an option of choosing one over the other. That way of viewing life on the planet simply exacerbates the fragmentation of the created order – it disintegrates – whereas salvation, the salvation of the world, is concerned with integration, with the restoration of wholeness.

> The salvation of which the Gospel speaks and which is determinative of the nature and function of the church is – as the very word itself should teach us – a making whole, a healing . . . the restoration of the harmony between man and God, between man and nature for which all things were created.[2]

What are the issues of spirituality, then, for apostolic people as they seek to fulfil the mandate to heal the sick, raise the dead, cleanse the lepers and drive out the demons? A great deal of helpful material already exists on the ministry of healing in all its various forms. I want to highlight three issues that may be important when we consider apostolic action in the world. They are, first, the issue of what we might call 'assertiveness', secondly, the possibility of rejection and, thirdly, the need to recognize the provisional character of all Christian healing.

The character of assertiveness

The biblical location of the dis-ease of the world is in the concept of 'fall', of the *intrusion* into the world of moral corruption, which has fragmented the inherent unity of the cosmic order. While the Old Testament is ambiguous about the origin and meaning of suffering[3] and even of evil,[4] the overriding impression of the New Testament witness, originating in the ministry of Jesus, is that sickness and death are intruders, enemies to the will of God. Thus Jesus in his ministry exerts authority over demons (Mark 1.25), over disease (Luke 4.39), over nature (Matthew 8.26), over death (Luke 7.14,15) and over sin (Luke 5.20). Again we are reminded of the breadth of God's healing. 'There is', says Bosch, 'in Jesus' ministry, no tension between saving from sin and saving from physical ailments, between the spiritual and the social.'[5]

The question of deliverance from sickness, disease and evil raises the issue of the potentially *assertive* nature of healing in the face of destructive powers. So, for example, in Mark 1, Jesus deals sternly with the evil spirit and is moved by a powerful emotion of compassion in the healing of the leper. This ability to engage his emotions in healing, to allow himself to be moved to action in the face of evil and suffering, would appear to be a key factor in advancing the kingdom. He allows himself to move out from himself towards the other. This is the engagement of the whole person in a hand-to-hand conflict with unquestionably strong powers, an engagement that requires mental strength, spiritual sinew and inner nerve. It is an action that is primarily *involved* rather than detached. It is full of resolve; it is risky. It is the antithesis of the kind of passivity with which, it could be argued, so much of Western Christianity views both structural evil and personal suffering.

Not placating but expelling

In a helpful analogy, Harvey Cox highlights the contrast between the traditional African approach to deliverance and that of the praying Christian, a contrast that he describes as having 'far-reaching implications, not only for African Christianity, but . . . for the role of religion in the twenty-first century':

> The divergence is that while the *nganga* tries to *placate* the evil spirit . . . the Christian prophet simply prays to the Holy Spirit to defeat and expel the intruder. While the *nganga* attempts to find out what the malignant spirits want, and then to satisfy them so they will go away, the prophet banishes them in the name of the Spirit of God and assures the sick person that he or she need no longer fear the spirits' powers since God's Spirit is mightier.[6]

Apostolic action requires engagement. The missionary journey is essentially a journey *out* towards the world. But it is not an aimless journey. It is the way in which the kingdom 'has been forcefully advancing' (Matthew 11.12). I realize that this phrase may upset or offend, as though the missionary journey were some kind of militaristic campaign or attempt to impose a given culture on another. It is not intended to give that impression. The assertive character of missionary spirituality must not be confused with aggression or harshness. The disarming of the powers is through the power of love. Nevertheless, when the journey begins to be taken seriously, there has to be a serious engagement with what is found 'out there'. All is not well in the world, and as apostolic people, we are required to engage with the world's sickness – however that sickness is expressed. That will inevitably lead to the requirement that we get our hands dirty – and sometimes the struggle will be very dirty indeed. The powers don't always shift easily.

The challenge for any Christian group is to look outside itself, into the pain of the world as it impacts upon their locality or network and ask, 'Is there anything we should be doing about this?' Until fairly recently, it was frequently assumed that the statutory services of the state were there to take care of the pain. The downside of this has meant that the local Christian community has often felt detached, helpless, uncertain about whether or not to respond to local need. It has even meant, at times, a kind of passive acceptance of the status quo. Now all that is changing and faith groups are increasingly responding to need in their communities. (Of course, the Christian community needs to discern which part(s) of 'out there' it is being called to engage with at any given time, and then to ask who its partners are.) When a PCC or a leadership team dares to ask the question, 'Is there anything we should be doing about this?', a kind of internal movement of faith, of belief, is generated. This develops into the belief that when we are faced with apparently intractable problems (drugs in the community, loneliness, vandalism, the needs of the disabled, children's play areas), the power of the gospel can always open up new possibilities, and that working with God, we can see a real transformation of lives and communities. This was the experience of the teams of mainly young people who moved to and lived on local authority estates in Manchester.

The Eden Project, Manchester

The idea was to form partnerships with a local church on an estate and to move in teams working at two levels. The first is 4 full time paid schools workers. They work in youth clubs, detached youth work, schools and with the Eden Bus Project. The second tier are up to 30 younger adults with secular jobs, working for Eden and the local church in a voluntary capacity, who would both disciple youth converts and be an incarnational presence on the estate. Both groups, by definition, move to and live on the estates where they work.

The dream is for 10 Eden projects on Manchester inner city estates, with 300 workers living long term as salt and light in their communities, working in conjunction with local churches or, where the church is notably weak, to bring in a partner church plant. 10 estates have been identified, 6 projects are running and 2 more are planned.

[There are many challenges.]

Hayden and Stuart have faced the challenge of walking into a literally empty council house, without gas and electricity connected . . . there is noise at night, people having open domestic conflicts, the higher prospect of being a victim of crime and instantly being spotted as 'one of those Christians – or Eden people' . . . as one person put it, 'You really do have to go out on cold wintry nights, it's totally sacrificial and you will be out of your comfort zone. It is hard work and I think we need to be honest about that sometimes.'[7]

The possibility of rejection

In the struggle with 'the powers' there is always the possibility that the messenger will be rejected. The act of intrusion into the world's settled arrangements is not always welcomed. 'I am sending you out like sheep among wolves,' promises Jesus (Matthew 10.16). Apostolic people are invited to identify with him through rejection and hostility. In fact, the proclamation may be more clearly heard through the patient bearing of hostility. As W. Klaiber says: 'What the messenger experiences and suffers can become the medium of understanding so that they are part of the proclamation.'[8]

For many Christians the question of weakness and smallness in the face of sometimes powerful negative forces can produce feelings of confusion and uncertainty, even loss of confidence. We feel that if we were 'better' at evangelism, could speak fluently about our faith, were less stumbling when it comes to witness, could be seen to be on top of life's problems, had more forceful characters and/or more sparkling personalities, looked better, were more attractive – then people might be persuaded to follow Christ. In fact, the apparent weakness and vulnerability, the ordinariness of apostolic people – being sheep among wolves – is absolutely necessary for the mission.

> It belongs to the essence [of the Christian faith] that it needs
> the weak witness, the powerless representative of the
> message. The people who are to be won and saved should, as
> it were, always have the possibility of crucifying the witness of
> the gospel.[9]

The weakness, the apparent lack of 'power', places the apostolic person or community into a rightfully vulnerable position. This is particularly important when considering mission among Western, twenty-first-century people. Thanks to television and mass media, most people have some smattering of understanding about basic psychology, about 'how power works', and how forces such as coercion and manipulation can operate in politics, religion and the family. They are street-wise and wary and on their guard against anything that might smack of spiritual abuse – and rightly so. So though it may feel uncomfortable, 'powerlessness' is absolutely essential in order to maintain the integrity of the message. It shifts the dynamic of sharing the good news away from a proclamation 'from above', to a speaking or acting on an equal level, or 'from below'. It places the missionary into the power of 'the other' and, in so doing, removes from the action of evangelism any possibility of coercion or use of force. Those who receive the message do not need to be dazzled or bludgeoned into hearing it. That wouldn't be the true message as we've received it. And powerlessness on the part of the messenger leaves those hearing or receiving the good news with plenty of freedom to respond or not. Isn't it time to celebrate our powerlessness rather than to rue it? For when we can accept our powerlessness as part of the deal, we are free to love.

Free to love

It has already been remarked that one of the aspects of the missionary journeys of Jesus is that he conducted much of his healing – as well as his teaching – ministry in the context of a circle of criticism and hostility. What was it that made him able to minister with freedom in such a context? Wasn't one reason because of the knowledge that he was 'greatly beloved'? A decision to trust God's committed and personal love, a love that holds us through trial and danger, must lie at the heart of the risk-taking of the gospel imperative. We are free to love. There is not always safety on the streets but there can be the ability to continue to love in the face of misunderstanding and persecution. That means facing fear. For some that will mean dealing with issues of personal safety, and with the kinds of questions that can be raised for local church communities when they start 'moving out'.

A common fear, one that still cripples many Christians, is that of public identification with Christ. This may not be obvious on a Sunday, but Sunday is not where most Christians spend their lives. Yet 'owning Christ publicly', being known as a follower and as a believer, actually releases, not only masses of reserves of energy for mission, but also a kind of interior freedom and joy. It is always good to be known for who you are. 'The people wept' when the Book of the Law was read publicly (Nehemiah 8); as Brueggemann puts it, 'The long season was finally past, an acknowledgment that our conventional consensus about the world no longer contradicts our own core identity. One becomes exhausted by faking it, in the massive pretence of being someone other than one really is.'[10] Perhaps some of our exhaustion, individual and corporate, comes from faking it? If so, we might find that a missional spirituality will assist the Church in England to move from faking it to freedom.

A robust spirituality

Missionary engagement therefore needs to draw on a particularly robust spirituality, which can take on the powers, whether social or supernatural.

It is, as we have seen, assertive and engaged. The roots of that assertive character are found, not in ourselves, but in the authority that has been given to us: 'heal . . . raise . . . cleanse . . . drive out . . .'

Christians have a right, in the name of Christ, to intrude into what has been called elsewhere 'the world's settled arrangements'.[11] We have a right to 'be', not just in our own communities but also in the public arena. Our presence and our actions are in the name of Jesus the Lord. Living under the lordship of Christ is an essential factor in possessing and maintaining this robustness, as the seven sons of Sceva – to whom we have already referred – found out (Acts19.13-16). Any church becoming mission-shaped must come to terms with this authority and the responsibility that such authority carries. Not that we are to be heavily burdened with a sense of self-importance. But we are called to grow up and to take our place in the secular *polis*. And one of the great gifts to the church that does this is a consequent growth, not in self-importance, but in self-respect. For isn't it true that taking hold of responsibility grows us up fast and that we end up liking ourselves better? And wouldn't liking ourselves better be good for the Church? Who knows but that helping to heal some of the world's woe might also help to heal some of our own?

Healing and its provisional nature

The relationship, therefore, between mission and healing is a vital one. Healings – ecological, communal, individual – are signs of the kingdom: 'If I drive out demons by the Spirit of God, then the kingdom of God has come upon you' (Matthew 12.28). Healings are what Roland Allen has called 'sermons in act',[12] words of the kingdom written in the stuff of biological and natural life. The fact that they are termed 'signs' highlights their provisional character. However good they may be, they are not ends in themselves but pointers towards the greater reality of the kingdom, whose agent is the Christ. Because of this they often have a temporary character. There may, for example, be a succession of physical healings at the start of a church plant, or some new work, that attract much local attention and draw some to faith. Margaret was another person whose healing had a great effect at the start of a new phase in a church's life.

Margaret's story

Everyone loved Margaret. She was married, with two sons, and worked in the offices of Sheffield Wednesday football club. She was in her 40s when she was diagnosed with ovarian cancer. The local doctor referred her to the curate at the church[13] and he went to visit her. Naturally, in this first meeting, the young man was treading carefully. But Margaret knew exactly why she wanted to see him. 'Look,' she burst out suddenly, after some polite conversation, 'I'm going to die and I want to know God!'

Margaret began to come to church. She went from strength to strength. She joined a house group, and she was full of questions. She embraced God and his people with joy and vigour and enthusiasm. Her natural warmth became a massive vehicle for the Spirit. She told everyone, at work, in the community, her family, how she had found faith. Her symptoms disappeared. She was apparently well.

Margaret's transformation had a massive effect upon the church as well as the community: she became one of the foundation stones of the new work that was beginning there. After a year, she discovered that the cancer had reappeared – this time in her brain. Had she 'just' been in remission? We'll never know. When she began to go downhill, the churchwarden commented to the vicar, 'If we don't have a miracle, we're going to lose Margaret.' His wise and gentle reply was, 'You mean if we don't have another miracle . . .' Her last weeks were full of joy. She was still hungry to learn. 'Tell me something from the Bible,' she used to say to the churchwarden, who called almost every day. One promise in particular she loved, and it was to become greatly important to her: 'I the Lord thy God will hold thy right hand, saying unto thee, Fear not; I will help thee' (Isaiah 41.13 AV).

In spite of the fact that Margaret's cancer reoccurred, the church consistently and faithfully continued to pray for physical healing, sometimes to real effect – but not always. Two young single mums, both with dependent children, died in spite of faithful prayer on the part of the church. Most churches have similar experiences. They are painful times of learning, through which it seems we have to pass as we grow in Christian ministry. We learn to live with the puzzles, with the mystery, with the unanswered questions. The real test is very often whether we will continue to believe in the healing power of God's love in the face of great disappointment and distress.

The temporary, random, uncontrollable character of signs serves also as a good reminder to us to beware of equating the signs with the kingdom. Signs don't signify arrival. One of the problems with apostolic activity is that there has frequently been, in the history of Christian mission, the temptation to assume that 'this' equals 'that'. We must be wary of any attempt to identify the signs too closely with the kingdom that is coming. We need to recognize that at the doorway of every power encounter there crouches, for a weak humanity, the possibility of megalomania. Too, the signs cannot be controlled or manipulated. They are freely given, and thus they require reservoirs of humble dependence upon God.

The very ambiguity of 'sign', the 'now and not yet' nature of the healing ministry, its apparent randomness, will also serve as a reminder to the apostolic person of his or her own brokenness and need for healing. Ministering the freedom of Christ is to be done by those who know that they, too, are recipients of that freedom. Acceptance of one's humanity, of strength and weakness, and a patient bearing with the pains and weaknesses of the human psyche with all its contradictions, is an essential part of a missionary spirituality that seeks to reach out and embrace the broken and the lost places of the world.

10 Learning, laughing and the long haul

'When the apostles returned, they reported to Jesus what they had done. Then he took them with him and they withdrew by themselves.'

Luke 9.10

Moving out in mission is never going to be easy or a quick fix – and that certainly proved true in the case of the Stepping Stones Church in North Anston, Sheffield.

A baptism of fire

The early months were uphill from day one. The heating system was found to be broken and condemned in January. Significantly disruptive children from the estate came, without their parents, partly attracted by the breakfast, sometimes on offer beforehand. Many of the weekly meetings of the team, now of 17, were difficult and the apparent unity of the start was shown to be shallow and short lived. By April only 8 of the 17 remained, but 4 further members of St James (the planting church) had come and stayed. The pain, cost, disappointment and discouragement all round can easily be appreciated. Already tired by hard work and conflict, the remaining group felt stretched and under resourced for the enormity of the task.

Yet somehow after that baptism of fire, despite mistakes, problems and disagreements, a greater sense of unity and togetherness emerged amidst the hard graft of running all-age worship and coping with all too human relationships.[1]

The roller-coaster story of this young church plant was to continue. For eighteen months (January 1998 to July 1999) it looked as though they had hit rock bottom. But gradually things began to change. From 1999, they turned a corner, with the appointment of Paul and Sheelagh Easby, both Church Army evangelists, to lead the young church. The church is still vulnerable – but it's there, and it's now recognized as the church in the community of Woodlands Drive.

Keeping on keeping on

One of the big questions for a mission-shaped church, and clearly one that Stepping Stones had to deal with, is the question of sustainability. It is one thing to launch out into a new venture. The enthusiasm, the sense of call, the feeling of adventure provide a terrific 'charge', which can carry us along for several months, if not some years. But what happens when it becomes clear that it's going to take a lot longer than we imagined? When we thought we'd gone to reap but actually find that we're doing the back-breaking work of picking stones out of the ground before we can even plant? What helps apostolic people to keep going? Where will fresh expressions of church find their resources for the long haul? How are we going to help people, especially young people involved in mission, with the kind of disappointment that can set in when it doesn't quite work out in the way we had imagined? And what do we do with the inevitable experiences of failure in our mission work, where we misjudge people, misread the culture, damage the cause of Christ by our clumsiness? Or when the thing runs out of steam, a key leader moves on, the pioneering group disappears, the original charisma seems to depart and the whole venture goes flat?

Michael Moynagh, in his book *emergingchurch.intro*, reminds us of how vulnerable even the most promising fresh expressions of church can be:

> The initiative by St Michael's, Blackheath . . . seemed poised to flourish . . . But soon afterwards its leader, Conrad Parsons, left. A member of the St Michael's congregation was appointed on a one-day-a-week basis to continue the work. But he was distracted by difficulties at home and in his work. The venture stalled. It now limps along, a mere whimper of what seemed possible a few years back.[2]

Questions concerning sustainability are going to be high on the agenda for diocesan and district officers as they seek to encourage fresh expressions of church. I want to highlight four issues to do with sustainability – the question of rhythm, shaking the dust, reporting back, and learning to rest.

Rhythms of return

First, there is the place of rhythm. If you make the journey up to the mother house of the Northumbria Community, you discover that the grey, lichened house is situated within a few miles of the sea. The holy island of Lindisfarne lies just across the waters and this close relationship to the sea and to Cuthbert's island retreat – the place of return – provides the community with natural models for their life and ministry.

The rhythms of the tides emphasize to the community the vital balance for them of 'the cell' and 'the coracle':

> As the tide draws upon the waters
> close in upon the shore
> make me an island
> set apart,
> alone with you, God,
> Holy to you.

> Then with the turning of the tide
> prepare me to carry your presence
> to the busy world that rushes in on me
> till the waters come again
> and fold me back to you.[3]

And the island retreat and the missionary journeys of Cuthbert remind the community of the need for 'home-coming' – a rhythm of going out and coming in that is formalized in their liturgy:

> May the peace of the Lord Christ go with you
> wherever he may send you.
> May he guide you through the wilderness,
> protect you through the storm.

> May he bring you home rejoicing
>> at the wonders he has shown you.
> May he bring you home rejoicing
>> once again into our doors.[4]

For Martin Garner, a Church Army captain who is working with teams of young people in mission in Sheffield, 'rhythm is vital'.[5] He describes it as three-fold – sowing and watching, reaping with energy, and 'keeping' – folding people in, building up community. This corresponds to the three-fold vision of the church he is attached to (St Thomas's, Crookes, in the Diocese of Sheffield), which has as its core value the maintenance of the balance between 'up, in and out', that is, the balance between God, one another and the world. 'Up-in-out' may sound like shorthand, but it's a useful way to check the balances in a church's common life.

It is from St Thomas's, Crookes, that the Order of Mission has developed, with a pattern of life expressed through five common daily times of prayer. This is just one of the expressions of a 'new monasticism' – another is the Northumbria Community –described by *Mission-shaped Church* as incorporating a variety of movements, groups and enthusiasms.[6] It is important to note that a rhythmical and structured prayer life is becoming increasingly valued by young Christians, many of whom have not grown up 'in church'.

One of the things about rhythm is that it connects us to something that is already there. It is not about our imposing a structure upon ourselves, but is about finding, getting in tune with, a pattern that already exists, deep down in the heart of things. Life in the Western world at the beginning of the twenty-first century militates against this discovery, but people of prayer have often stumbled upon the secret – when they start living rhythmically they begin to be connected to something that can be life-renewing to them. This is one of the great strengths, of course, of following a liturgical calendar. But the rhythm is not only concerned with a structured prayer life. It is about knowing when to 'hunker down', to close the door, to switch off the phone, to go for a walk, to say 'no'. It's about discovering the things that make for peace for us. Many who live mostly in the left brain as well as the fast lane will find that digging potatoes, fixing the car, playing football, dancing to music, preparing a meal, repainting the spare room begin to put them in touch with those deeper patterns. Physical labour – so valued by the Benedictines, often so misunderstood and denigrated by our present culture – can reconnect us to the earth and to lost rhythms.

Other rhythms of life also need balancing. Mission may lead us into dark and painful places but we still must celebrate life: we need parties and picnics as well as prayer.

Shaking the dust

To twenty-first-century Christians, 'shaking the dust' (Matthew 10.14; Luke 9.5; Luke 10.10-12) may appear nothing more than an archaic bit of ritual, but it can highlight for us another issue in how to manage sustainability.

The action, understood by biblical scholars as a prophetic action, finds resonance in the material in Ezekiel 33.1-6 as well as elsewhere in the New Testament. We get a clue into how it can be useful to us by Tannehill's description of it as 'a solemn sign of separation'.[7] For the question of separation is crucial, both for the messengers and the hearers of the good news. There is a subtle demarcation between responsibilities.

> After having explained God and Jesus Christ to the people,
> I had come to the end of the good news. It might seem a bit
> abrupt, but I believe it is true. After proclaiming all that God
> has done in the world because of his love for the world and
> for human beings, and after announcing the depths to which
> this love has gone in the person and love of Jesus Christ, the
> missionary's job is complete. What else is there? . . . The rest is
> up to the people hearing the message. They can either reject
> the message entirely, or they can accept it. If they accept it,
> what they must do is outlined in general in scripture, but that
> outline should not be considered part of the good news.
> I think it is rather the response to the good news. It is the
> church.[8]

For the messenger, there is the responsibility of imparting the message, but there the responsibility ends. The *response* is purely the rightful responsibility of the other. There is a rightful demarcation between the two. The missionary task is to proclaim – not to convert. Conversion (a turning, a change of mind, a change of life direction) is properly to do with the one who responds. This is wonderfully freeing for both parties. For the missionary, it means freedom from anxiety about 'results'; for the other, it means freedom to respond, without fear of being manipulated. When evangelism takes place within this kind of freedom-field, the task is transformed. Even if nothing is specifically said, people sense when this freedom is operating. And they relax. So do those who are doing the evangelizing. That makes the whole encounter more satisfying – for both parties.

This quality of detachment should not be confused with walking away when the going gets tough. The going will be very tough at times and part of the cost of mission and ministry is staying there, continuing to love and to serve, in the face of hostility or complete lack of interest. We saw how the Stepping Stones plant in Anston, Sheffield, managed to hang on in there: George Lings, commenting on the story of Stepping Stones, says this:

> Unless an incoming planting community, with continuity of leadership, is there for the long haul, it may be almost better not to start. Short-term work will only raise temporary expectations, but disappoint long-term transformation. Pulling out at the down time, which will follow short-term investment, carries damaging implications. It means another failure of the Church's mission to the urban poor; and another unwelcome experiment on the local community. This in turn further hardens the ground for any subsequent seed sowers.[9]

Mission is not about walking away: but it is about trying to be relaxed about 'outcomes'. A certain amount of detachment is essential. If you want good fruit, don't keep plucking at it. We'll bruise the young fruit if we handle it too much. When we stop being detached, we start getting destructive. Detachment is not only for the sake of those to whom the mission is directed but is also for the missionaries themselves.

> True spirituality in mission depends on the maintenance of a proper balance between God's sovereign and all-embracing redemptive purpose and our human responsibility . . . If our activism focuses on the level of response . . . it soon degenerates into frenetic and manipulative activity.[10]

Frenetic and manipulative activity is deeply destructive to the church. It is often a sign that we have stopped trusting in the work of the Holy Spirit in the life of those to whom we are sent. We don't have to make the thing happen. God is in the picture, too. Detachment helps us let go, and when we let go we can enjoy trusting. It isn't all up to us – he has other agents, and other agencies of the Spirit out there.

Recognizing impermanence

Further, to balance what has already been said about 'staying there', we probably also need to recognize that some mission endeavour will have a necessary impermanence. Mass at Asda (page 25) initiated by Fr Damian, came to a natural end in autumn 2000. But it had done its work of sowing. Some projects will have a brief life: they will affect a few lives and then those people move on and affect a few more. That may be particularly true where projects are related to 'culture' – given that the culture changes at such a rate. We need wisdom to discern when to let go and when to hang on. Sometimes in our churches we have hung on too long to initiatives. People have a vision for something, we set it up, it is fruitful, but then years later, decades even, we are still keeping it going, even when there is every indication that the Spirit – and the culture – has moved on. It can be an important – and freeing – lesson for a church leadership to allow itself to question why it is still doing some of the things it is doing!

Reporting back

Thirdly, there is the issue of what the biblical account calls 'reporting back'. Reporting back is all part of return. It includes a permissible celebration at the success of the mission (Luke 10.17): nowhere do we gather any sense of disapproval on the part of Jesus at what some might label triumphalism. We are allowed to celebrate the growth of the church. It is not in bad taste to be glad when people come home to God. The celebration is more costly, of course, when it's not 'our' church that's grown, or 'our' tradition that for the moment is seeing the prodigals come home.

But reporting back is not all about celebration. It's about beginning to make sense of what has been happening out there in mission. There is the opportunity for reflection. The seventy-two look back over what they have seen and heard on the mission field, and Jesus helps them to think theologically about it – 'I saw Satan fall like lightning from heaven' (Luke 10.18). This helps to build up their grasp of the kind of authority they have been given – and also to warn of some of the inherent dangers: Don't rejoice that the spirits give way to you – don't start investing your identity in *that*, that won't get you anywhere – instead, invest it in *this* – that your names, you yourselves, are known by the Father (Luke 10.20). They are apprentices, learning the lessons of mission. They do it by coming back and talking it over together and with Jesus. Churches that are beginning to engage in mission, however small and tentative, must ensure that the opportunity for reflection is built in to the exercise.

Reporting back is also to do with accountability. 'Eternity' is a youth church, and one expression of the mission of St Michael's, Warfield, in Berkshire. Mark Weardon welcomes the structure of accountability with the sending church:

> The most important thing is that keeping within our mother church is imperative. Being accountable is so necessary. We would not have gone ahead with planting Eternity if we did not have 100% blessing from St Michael's. The prayer support, teaching and care from them is invaluable'.[11]

People who are engaged in church planting or any kind of missionary endeavour need to have opportunities for reflective learning – whether this is something they structure in themselves, or whether it is provided as a form of on-going support by the diocese or sending church.

Hearing what's happening

It [Pathway church plant, Nottingham] sounds good so far, but comments about lack of support from the sending church, coping with its own strains . . . indicated some important needs not being met. Having lay leaders with a participatory style, all of whom were in employment, seems good for heading off complaints, but led to members not wanting to admit pastoral needs for fear of over burdening the leaders. The fortnightly midweek groups, in

> theory offered the necessary pastoral support and input in
> spirituality but they were not that easy to join and it was the
> same small group of hard-working leaders who were the
> facilitators.
>
> The leaders were engagingly honest that after three years
> down the track, there was a concerning sense of plateau.
> Being in a rented building, the church having no corporate
> home and being led by spare timers made for a lack of
> leadership focus. The leaders were tired out by the required
> level of work. They felt inadequate to take the church any
> further forward, vision and energy were absent and exercising
> leadership was more difficult by being well-known fellow-
> members. Even Jesus struggled with ministry at Nazareth.

A hidden negative

Reflection on what has been really going on – what has been good and
what has been not so good, on lessons learned through failure as well as
success – is one of the most fruitful exercises that an apostolic church can
take part in. Yet it is also, at present, one of the most neglected. A great
many churches, of all kinds of traditions, from time to time engage in a piece
of evangelistic activity. A flurry of planning, the challenge of prayer
beforehand, the excitement of the event itself, are often not followed
by careful assessment. This is a great loss to the church and the wider
mission.

Sometimes a group of people set off on the adventure of church planting
only to find it fizzling out. Or a couple of people may try setting up a lunch-
time Christian gathering at work, only to find that it never really takes off.
Several of those kinds of experiences, without the chance of reflection and
learning – and the church or the individual will simply quietly give up
altogether. If the event has not produced the hoped-for results ('more
young people in church', 'more men') a subtext gets laid like a stone into the
foundation of the corporate psyche of the church – and of the vicar. The
subtext says something like this: 'We don't do evangelism, we are no good at
it. We'll stick to luncheon clubs, we do them well.' Often unspoken, often

unacknowledged, it can lie there, underneath, exerting power – a well-hidden negative. All that's left is sometimes a kind of wistfulness that we wish we *were* like that, or resentment or cynicism towards those who seem to succeed.

We have to have the courage to sit down together and really look at what we've done, what was good, what worked, what didn't work, and what we will do differently next time. We have to turn experiences of disappointment and apparent failure in mission, when they happen, into opportunities to learn. After all, if for 1,500 years the Church of England has been a settled Church, it's got a lot of learning to do. No skill is ever learned without sweat. Sitting together, reflecting together, is a great invigorator. It takes seriously the fact that this is a real task to be done, with real lessons to be learned. It takes seriously the potential in each individual and in each church for real growth to happen through them. It determines that the 'little ones', too, can be used in the Father's work (Luke 10.21). And it means that we don't give up at the first hurdle!

Resting

Finally, the need for rest is essential for sustainability: 'Then he took them with him and they withdrew by themselves . . .' (Luke 9.10).

The Franciscan Rule reminds us of the essential relationship between the renewal of life and mission: 'Without the constant renewal of divine grace the spirit flags, the will is weakened, the conscience grows dull, the mind loses its freshness and even the bodily vigour is impaired.'[12]

Paul Hamilton is a Church Army officer who went to Canvey Island in 1996. The story of some of the lessons he learned there is documented in *Encounters on the Edge*.

Cell on Canvey Island

As a young evangelist interested only in leading people to Christ, Paul admits he had a deficient, solely functional, view of church. Activism needed changing through deeper roots of spiritual disciplines, in particular prayer and fasting, now in a monthly pattern. Over time, St

Katherine's have found that when they sought numbers, they waned, but when they sought God, numbers came, too. The good idea and the God idea are not coterminous.

Paul began to suspect that God wanted to make the following clear: the reinvigorating of St Katherine's and the evangelization of fresh people would occur despite the lack of church resources . . . Paul began to spend time with a few core members, despite some criticism from others about favouritism and time given. They began meeting as a cell group, but two of the seven left the cell because, in their words, 'It is too much about God now' . . . however, the cell had a significant effect on the worship. In Paul's words: 'The thing that had failed to strike me in my naivety was that these people had to fall in love with Jesus again. They were drained and demoralized; they had tried everything new. So, in the small group I tried to help people fall in love with Jesus again and it worked well. This flowed into worship . . . all these people who had had their faith rekindled wanted to do was sing.'

[Eventually, the cell grew, then multiplied.] Cell on Canvey has been demystified and stands for Caring, Equipping, Learning and Laughing . . . Paul sees that the cell relational network has brought an emphasis on discipleship and reduced the drop-out rate from church.[13]

'Caring, equipping, learning and laughing' is an apt way of describing what is needful for long-term sustainability. Learning to rest, and learning how to allow other people to rest, assists in mission. Resting acknowledges our need of God and our need of recreation: it signals that we are not indispensable; it reconnects us to the source of our energy:

We know that a mature and integrated human person can combine a vast output of labour with a deep inner rest: indeed, one is the condition of the other . . . It is a rest which is held in tension with ceaseless labour, and the name of that tension is hope.[14]

Learning to rest means, too, that we accept that we are in for the long haul. It's about pacing ourselves. Rest has realism built into it. We are not machines, and a church whose officers and leaders encourage each other to operate like machines may be a church in great danger of being driven by unreal expectations fuelled by anxiety. It can be an important turning point for a church when the leadership begins to signal that 'rest' is a legitimate – and essential – part of the exercise.

Joyfully serious and seriously joyful

These images of rhythm and of returning-with-detachment, of reflection and of rest speak powerful words of freedom into the climate of anxiety that so often dominates our church culture with regard to mission. They mediate a kind of relaxed maturity about the mission, a sense of well-being, a light-heartedness about the whole enterprise. We are to be both joyfully serious and seriously joyful about the task. At the heart of this is surely a particular humility: a humility that recognizes that the outcome of the mission is God's not ours, that there is always much to learn and that the relationship of trust and dependence must constantly be attended to. We may die for the mission, but we are not to live for it – we are to live only for God.

11 An apostolic adventure

'"Come, follow me," Jesus said, "and I will make you fishers of [people]." At once they left their nets and followed him.'

Mark 1.17,18

What the Church of England could do with possibly more than anything else at present is an adventure. Settlement may have brought many blessings, but it has left us bored. And bored churches become boring churches. Western secular culture is also bored. When you've got everything, there's not a lot more to do, except to get more. The two things – the boredom of the Church and the boredom of the culture – are probably not unrelated. But what Christ calls us to is adventure. An adventure where the risks are real and the stakes are high. A big adventure, where there's no going back and where the outcomes are not predetermined. This adventure grows people up faster than anything else: it stretches them and pushes them into shapes they didn't know they could have. One of the discoveries they make along the way is that the stretching doesn't break them, it develops them: they grow to like themselves more and they become more confident.

The clergy may need adventure more than anyone else. Most – highly motivated, sensitive, passionate, caring, longing to be used effectively in the service of the gospel of God – signed up so that they could make a difference. Many of them believe they were called to an adventure with God. But the long years of toiling under the yoke of the expectations of 'settlement' – of managing buildings, of organizing the yearly round for the local church, of overseeing arrangements for 'bun fights' and bazaars – have, for some of us, led to a kind of servitude wherein not only does the idea of missionary adventure now seem dangerous but also abhorrent. From this perspective, the apostolic adventure can also appear, to the jaded minister, like 'just more hard work'. It's easier to keep doing what we've always done, mending the nets. That's hard work, and it's dull, but at least we can do it without too much thought. And while we're mending, we can always dream about adventure and about how it might have been, 'had things been different'.

But the hard work of the adventure of mission is not the same as the hard work of doing what we've always done. That's because, as I hope this book has suggested, the apostolic adventure is capable of generating massive internal energy. Anything that requires exercise, 'stretch', movement outwards, begins to generate heat, and the heat begins to affect, to warm up, the whole body. Too, the nets can look different from a distance. What looks terribly important today can, from another perspective, show itself as relatively trivial. And those nets that are important are discovered to be capable of renewal when harnessed back into the purpose for which they were originally designed.

It is one of the dynamics of faith that it requires action before sight. The man who was blind was told to go and wash in the pool of Siloam. 'So the man went and washed, and came home seeing' (John 9.7). It was as the lepers went that they were cleansed (Luke 17.14). It will surely be in the going, in following the Spirit of God into mission, that the Church is changed: the 'going out' will in fact press us 'deeper in' – because the heart of God goes out constantly from himself towards those who are still lost in the dark places of the earth. What will it mean for the Church to follow the Spirit into mission? What might it mean on the ground – for the local church? For ecumenical partners? What could it mean for a deanery?

Two things immediately spring to mind when thinking about the adventure of mission. One is the question of crossing boundaries. The other, related to boundary crossing, is about taking risks. It is these two that we shall explore briefly in this chapter.

Crossing boundaries

Mass at Asda

In Fr Damian's language, the Incarnate Christ was placed on a supermarket table (see p. 25); precious things and words were made available to all, including the careless. The paradoxical desire for Purity, which tends to separate, and for Incarnation, which crosses boundaries to join, met in the demonstration of the Holy.[1]

Jesus' own view of boundaries is striking in its ambiguity. He was deeply rooted in his own culture and took part in its cultic practices, appearing to accept the limits of the Torah as normative for his life. He also exercised the freedom to critique the interpretation of the Law.

He was highly focused on the limits of his own missionary calling: 'I was sent only to the lost sheep of Israel' (Matthew 15.24) and he imposed similar limits on the early missionary task of his followers: 'Do not go among the Gentiles or enter any town of the Samaritans' (Matthew 10.5). Yet he broke the 'rules of separation' all over the place. He ate with unwashed hands, partied with 'sinners', and entered the house of a tax collector whose job rendered him unclean. He asked a Samaritan woman for a drink (double jeopardy that!), he touched lepers, he healed on the Sabbath, he washed feet. We might even glimpse something of a paradigm shift in his thinking about his own calling and mission as he is confronted by a Canaanite woman, who feistily stands her ground in the face of his apparent rejection of her demand for help. Or is he literally teasing out her faith?

Taking risks

But it's the story of Peter and Cornelius that really begins to stretch the Early Church. It's easy for us who are familiar with the story in Acts 10 and 11 to skate over the accounts without stopping to meditate long and hard on the very great adventure across the cultural and social divide that the Church was required to make. They took a decision to step away from the cultural norms of their tradition, a decision which, it's worth noting, was based on some not entirely promising evidence: a vision on a hot roof at noon, some interesting coincidences, and an opportunity to preach, during which there was an ecstatic outpouring to God on the part of the hearers during the sermon. Somewhere, too, in the back of their minds as they came to their decision might have been old texts that suggested a breathtaking inclusiveness on the part of God, mixed with ambiguous statements that Jesus had made about going only to the lost sheep of the house of Israel, and to the ends of the earth.

Isn't it just this kind of wrestling and risk-taking that we need to reclaim? The church in Antioch was to take risks by sending out Paul and Barnabas. The church in Jerusalem struggled with the implications of a God accepting the Gentiles 'by giving the Holy Spirit to them, just as he did to us' (Acts 15.8). The acceptance, when it came, was cautious and not without conditions. But the caution should not blind us to the very significant risk-taking that was going on. Becoming an apostolic people, a people who were being sent, was beginning to bite. It was starting to affect those who were sent, as well as those to whom they were going. Former ways of understanding the world were being challenged through the missionary enterprise. It was all getting very much more dangerous.

Locked in with God – or locking him out?

I had been regaling some young colleagues with a rather entertaining story of a night out in a rough pub in Sheffield with some friends: how there had been a 'lock-in' at the end of the evening, and the way that the after-hours' conversation had turned to God. I described how this particular friendship had been developing over many years, how challenging it was and also how much I received from it. One of the young Christians who was listening to this story asked, 'But how do you avoid becoming "contaminated"?'

Reflecting on the conversation later, I was reminded of the very deep and primal fear of 'contamination' that lies at the heart of so much religion, and of the consequent erection of boundaries – moral, cultural, social, physical – that may have originally been for a good purpose but tend to take over as the dominant and defining structure of a particular faith community. Such boundaries can trap us in as well as keep others out. Or, to put it another way, a 'lock-in' in the Church might just mean some very stale air after a while!

By contrast, 'Thank you for making us holy', and, 'Thanks for not disapproving of the smell of beer on our breath' were two telling comments after midnight Mass in the local pub, the Anderton Arms, in the Longsands parish, Blackburn Diocese.[2]

Travelling into the unknown place

One of the greatest felt risks in the crossing of boundaries is the risk to oneself or one's community – when I cross a boundary I not only leave behind the familiar, but I may be changed through what I meet with on the other side. Indeed, the whole thrust of argument in *Mission-shaped Church* is strongly geared towards a willingness to 'let the shape and form of the new church be determined by the mission context for which it [is] intended'.[3] One leader described how crossing boundaries was beginning to change him: 'I have recognised the need to trust young people with leadership – to be much more of a coach and leader, rather than "doing" all the stuff for them.'[4]

We have already seen how the challenge to move out from ourselves in mission means that we must be deeply rooted in God: it would be a mistake to assume that 'being deeply rooted in God in mission' means that we will necessarily always *feel* secure. For there can be no going in mission without a certain amount of felt vulnerability and risk as we move out from the safe and the familiar, whether to plant a church in a house on a new estate, run a 'seekers group' in a pub, start a small after-school club, join with other faiths to address common community issues, do a soup run in the city centre at night, or take part in a local radio debate on matters of faith.

So one cross-cultural missionary, an ordained priest forming Christian community among unchurched people in Bristol, says: 'It has been unsettling. It has not been easy, leaving the structured expectations of clergy life and moving to a different area. It has been hard forming such relationships and quite turbulent as an experience.'[5] And another, the leader of Church Without Walls in Stoke, writes: 'My family and I are, undoubtedly, cross-cultural missionaries. We and our children have felt very different (like aliens!) from those we live amongst.'[6] 'A doorway to closeness'[7] is how one young woman, engaged through her local church in mission in Sheffield, describes the kind of vulnerability that goes with moving out towards others.

Risking offence and danger

The apostolic adventure, then, involves engaging with the costly and risky business of crossing boundaries. It may mean risking offending others in the tradition. It can feel dangerous. It is alert to the possibility of change ahead for the missionary endeavour: it cannot afford to be complacent. It means that what is and what isn't important has to be weighed up. Decisions have to be made, decisions that commit to a course of action – letting go of some things, retaining others, embracing the possibility of compromise. It means learning to seize hold of sudden opportunities and using them in the service of the gospel (see Acts 17.16-34), working responsively with what it finds 'out there'.

Apostolic hospitality and parish boundaries

But there are other boundaries to be crossed as well and 'knowing who you are before God and knowing yourself to be greatly loved' is also essential when boundary crossing happens in these other ways. *Mission-shaped Church* endorses the need for an Anglicanism that recognizes the three dimensions of territory, neighbourhood and network, and the different models of mission that are required by the different dimensions. It remains strongly committed to the parish model, while urging engagement with the other dimensions:

> It is clear to us that the parochial system remains an essential
> and central part of the national Church's strategy to deliver
> incarnational mission. But the existing parochial system alone is
> no longer able fully to deliver its underlying mission purpose.[8]

Thus, one of the greatest challenges that a new missionary paradigm brings to the Church of England is the prospect of increased church planting across parish boundaries, either into a physical location – such as on a particular estate – or among a particular people-group, such as night-clubbers or young office workers. And this permeability of parish boundaries can bring with it its own stresses and strains, often felt by the local parish church.

Anecdotal evidence suggests that such crossing of boundaries can leave a local church feeling bruised, and that church planting across boundaries is still regarded with suspicion and hostility by many local clergy and church congregations. There have been cases where threats of litigation and of the withdrawing of parish share have played a part in the negotiation of boundary crossing. One area dean wrote:

> From the 'host' church, feelings towards the plant may vary from mild disdain to outright hostility. There is often a lack of comprehension as to the reasons for the plant wanting to come into the parish: 'Why don't they come and work with us?' Or, 'Why don't they come and talk to us? We've been here for more than a century, who do they think they are? What do they know about this part of town? Why are we not good enough?'

He outlines other feelings too:

> Feelings of mistrust towards incomers and the diocese as a result of perceptions of 'done deals' brokered without any consultation . . . charges of insensitivity towards plant and hierarchy as a result of feeling ignored, excluded or overridden . . . a sense of impotence: 'We don't want these people in our parish but what can we do?' Feelings of resignation: 'We'll just carry on doing what we do anyway' . . . and feelings of being threatened: 'We struggle to pay our quota, the plant is only interested in cherry-picking people who could boost the life of our church.'

Feelings of being ignored, excluded, overridden, impotent, and threatened are deeply frightening and unpleasant. Whether or not the feelings are justified can only be known by those who are closely involved in the setting up, encouragement and brokerage of individual church plants. What is probably true, however, is that the temptation to adopt an insecure and basically fearful stance is one that is open to any church faced with an incoming missionary endeavour. What is equally likely is that the same experience may become a quarry through which the hard work of spirituality could yield a rich seam of spiritual maturity for the local church in terms of grace, generosity, hospitality and a secure sense of its own identity and place within the overall scheme of local apostolic activity.

We have already suggested that boundary crossing involves risk-taking. The story of St Saviour's, Sunbury, in the Diocese of London, is the story of a small, rather struggling congregation in the Anglo-Catholic tradition that dared to take a big risk. It's the story of the kind of 'dying to live' that undergirds the theology of *Mission-shaped Church*.[9]

 ### Their big chance

It was suggested to St Saviour's that they might consider receiving a 'transplant', a sizeable group of people, from a thriving evangelical church (St Stephen's, Twickenham) in another deanery. There was a great deal of consternation about this, and not a little resistance. People threatened to leave. But then 86-year-old Beryl Wildrig spoke up. Beryl was the churchwarden and had attended church for 60 years. She, with others, had been praying for the day the church would grow. She said that this was their big chance. It proved to be a 'Simeon' moment for the church. The PCC voted unanimously to accept the planting team.

Because the PCC embraced and welcomed the new group, there wasn't the mass exodus that had been threatened. Now the church building has gone from being open a few hours a week to being open most days and for many hours, and with hundreds of people attending the midweek drop-in work, it is fast becoming an important centre for building community in Sunbury. The church has developed cell groups – 13 of them at present – and they have just stated a second Sunday service in 'café style'. At the time of writing (spring 2006) they are just about to have a Church Weekend Away with 140 people attending. And Beryl? She died just a few weeks after that momentous meeting, but as the present vicar commented, 'She had made sure the ground was set for the future of her church.'

At heart, the kinds of issues that St Saviour's, Sunbury, chose to face and work with are issues of spirituality, and the church that can face them head on, work with them and make something good from them is a church that is learning just as much as the missionaries how to be an 'apostolic church'. Allowing the mission to happen on 'our' patch, affirming it when it goes well, praying publicly for its leaders, speaking only positively about it in public, is something that requires the generous and open-heartedness of true Christian character.

This is much more than 'putting a brave face on it'. We can be hugely appreciative of the tradition we are part of while at the same time recognizing the validity of those of other Christians. We know enough about the spirituality of different personality types to recognize that people may respond to different traditions of the Church at different stages of their spiritual journeys. It is a truly apostolic church that recognizes and affirms this: it is a generous and mature priest or mission leader who will say to a seeker, 'I think that what you seem to be needing at this stage is the kind of spirituality that you will find at St Agatha's/the local church plant/the Methodists down the road.' Can the churches of the Church of England and its leaders rise to a challenge such as this or are we bound to inhabit for ever a default mode of defensiveness and entrenchment?

Following the Spirit into adventure

The price of adventure might be high, but the rewards can be great. For whereas a ghetto mentality shrinks human persons, the 'stretch' of adventure brings enlargement – an enlargement of the human person, an enlargement of vision, an enlargement in confidence. The adventure of mission has no secure outcomes: the journey has to be made without knowing the destination. We are not without support – we have a compass, bread for the journey and each other. And we have lessons already being learned. But we are nevertheless heading to an unknown place and, in company with many who have gone before us, we can rely only on the Holy Spirit to show us the way. Such dependence on the Spirit would accord well with the first generation of seventeenth-century Quakers at Balby in Doncaster, who, to encourage those who would follow them, wrote:

> We do not want you to copy or imitate us.
> We want to be like a ship that has crossed the ocean,
> leaving a wake of foam, which soon fades away.
> We want you to follow the Spirit, which we have sought
>   to follow,
> but which must be sought anew in every generation.[10]

It might just be that we are beginning to get an indication of where the Spirit is leading us in our present generation. For when making preparations for any big expedition, it can be useful, if not essential, to make some initial forays – to look at the lie of the land, to provide information, to relay detailed reports about 'how it is out there' back to those at home so that adjustments can be made, and structures be put in place, to manage the main task. The bigger the adventure, the greater the need for careful preparation. Everest has to be climbed in several stages – five times altogether – up to the place from which the final ascent is to be made. Camps have to be built, ropes fixed in place, supplies taken up, before the last push to the summit. Perhaps the Spirit is nudging us through the voices from those already making forays in mission in our culture – whether using traditional models of mission or fresh expressions? Perhaps, then, we need to take those voices very seriously indeed, to learn from them, from their mistakes as well as their joys – and to begin to harness the lessons learned from the small stories in preparation for the bigger venture that clearly lies ahead.[11]

That venture will take nothing less than a prolonged, thoughtful, concerted and united effort, not just by the Anglican Church, but also by the Churches together, if we are to bring the good news of God's saving love to our present generation – and the generations to come. It will require everything we've got – and then, even then, the outcome won't necessarily be the one that might be expected. After all, isn't that the risk, and the exhilaration, of true adventure?

Notes

About the book

1. Church of England Mission and Public Affairs Council, *Mission-shaped Church*, Church House Publishing, 2004.
2. Commission of the Church Assembly, *Towards the Conversion of England*, Church Assembly Press, 1945, p. 2.
3. *Mission-shaped Church*, p. 85.
4. William Abraham, *The Logic of Evangelism*, Eerdmans, 1989, p. 95.

Chapter 1

1. *Mission-shaped Church*, p.12.
2. *Mission-shaped Church*, p.12.

Chapter 2

1. *Mission-shaped Church*, p.85.
2. Gordon Crowther, questionnaire, June 2004.
3. Contributor at a workshop at *Mission 21*, Sheffield, 2006.
4. George Lings, *Encounters on the Edge*, No. 4, the Sheffield Centre, pp. 7, 8.
5. Conversation with author on 10 March 2006.
6. Walter Brueggemann, *Biblical Perspectives on Evangelism*, Abingdon Press, 1993, p. 90.
7. Andrew Walker, *Telling the Story: Gospel, mission and culture*, SPCK, 1996, p. 48.
8. Lesslie Newbigin, *The Household of God*, SCM Press, 1953, p. 29.

Chapter 3

1. www.somewhereelse.co.uk
2. Dr and Mrs Howard Taylor, *Biography of James Hudson Taylor*, Hodder & Stoughton, 1973, p.148.
3. *Biography of James Hudson Taylor*, p. 149.
4. T. S. Eliot, 'The Journey of the Magi', *Selected Poems*, Faber & Faber, 1961.
5. Baz Gascoigne, contribution to a workshop at *Mission 21*, Sheffield, 2006.
6. Linda Edge, Stepping Stones, Sheffield Diocese.
7. Contribution to a workshop at *Mission 21*, Sheffield, 2006.
8. Members of the Julian Shrine, *Enfolded in Love: Daily readings with Julian of Norwich*, Darton, Longman & Todd, 1980, p. 39.

Chapter 4

1. Jürgen Moltmann, *The Open Church*, Fortress Press, 1978, p. 23.
2. Council for Mission and Public Affairs, *Mission-shaped Church,* Church House Publishing, 2004, p. 90.
3. George Lings, *Encounters on the Edge*, No. 16, the Sheffield Centre, 2002, pp.10f.
4. *Mission-shaped Church*, p. 13.
5. *Encounters on the Edge*, No. 26, 2005, p. 7.
6. *Mission-shaped Church*, p.105.
7. Attributed to Eugene Peterson.
8. George G. Hunter III, *How to Reach Secular People*, Abingdon Press, 1992, p. 108.
9. *Encounters on the Edge*, No. 11, p. 21.
10. *Encounters on the Edge*, No. 21, 2004, pp. 2–4.
11. The Revd Nick Crawley, interview with author on 1 June 2005.

Chapter 5

1. See, for example, J. C. Fenton, *The Gospel of Matthew*, Penguin, 1963, p.186.
2. Council for Mission and Public Affairs, *Mission-shaped Church*, Church House Publishing, 2004, p. 30.
3. Alan Kreider, *Worship and Evangelism in pre-Christendom*, Grove, 1995, p. 34.
4. *Worship and Evangelism*, p. 15.
5. Margaret Caunt, now team vicar of St Peter's, Gleadless, Sheffield Diocese.
6. Cited in John Stott (ed.), *Making Christ Known*, Paternoster Press, 1996, p. 148.
7. Walter Brueggemann, *Biblical Perspectives on Evangelism*, Abingdon Press, 1993, p. 10.
8. *Biblical Perspectives*, p. 11.
9. Andrew Allington, vicar, St Mary's Stainforth, Doncaster.
10. *Mission-shaped Church*, p. 105.
11. Laurence Keith, 'How we went and had to let go', 2006.
12. Vincent Donovan, *Christianity Rediscovered*, SCM Press, 1982, p. 81.
13. Mark Tanner, vicar, St. Mary, Doncaster, conversation on 10 March 2006.

Chapter 6

1. Netherhall Community Church, Doncaster.
2. David W. Shenk and Ervin R. Stuzman, *Creating Communities of the Kingdom*, Herald Press, 1988, p. 42.
3. Steven Croft, *Transforming Communities*, Darton, Longman & Todd, 2002, p. 71.
4. Council for Mission and Public Affairs, *Mission-shaped Church*, Church House Publishing, 2004, p. 52.
5. Cited by Shenk of Hiebert's theory, *Creating Communities*, p. 103.
6. George Lings, *Encounters on the Edge*, No. 19, the Sheffield Centre, pp. 10–14.
7. *Encounters on the Edge*, No. 20, pp. 13, 14.

Chapter 7

1. Now vicar of St Mary's, Doncaster.
2. *Northumbria Community – A Way for Living*, undated, p. 5.
3. Martin Garner, 2002.
4. Questionnaire, Jesus Fellowship Church member, 2002.
5. St Thomas's, Wincobank, Sheffield.
6. Author's own story!
7. C. S. Lewis, *The Lion, The Witch and the Wardrobe*, Lion Publications, 1980, p. 75.
8. Questionnaire, 2003.
9. David and Jane Johnson, then in York Diocese.
10. Helen Waddell (trans.), *The Desert Fathers*, Constable, 1936, p. 157.
11. John Kelleher, questionnaire, June 2005.
12. Cited by Kenneth Leech, *True God*, Sheldon Press, 1985, p. 148.

Chapter 8

1. Lesslie Newbigin, *A Faith For This One World*, Wyvern Books, 1965, p. 48.
2. Written testimonial, member of St Thomas's Church, Wincobank.
3. Laurence Keith, 'How we went and had to let go', 2006.
4. George Lings, *Encounters on the Edge*, No. 7, the Sheffield Centre, p. 11.
5. Professor Roy Greenslade in an interview on Radio 4, 11 August 2005.

Chapter 9

1. Katherine Francis, reader, St Thomas's Church, Wincobank, Sheffield.
2. Lesslie Newbigin, *The Household of God*, SCM Press, 1964, p. 140.
3. 'I am the Lord, and there is no other.
   I form the light and create darkness,
   I bring prosperity and create disaster;
   I, the LORD, do all these things' (Isaiah 45.6-7).
4. 'And the Lord God said, "The man has now become like one of us, knowing good and evil"' (Genesis 3.22).
5. David Bosch, *Transforming Mission*, Orbis, 1991, p. 33.
6. Harvey Cox, *Fire From Heaven*, Cassell, 1996, pp. 255–6.
7. George Lings, *Encounters on the Edge*, No.14, The Sheffield Centre, 2002, pp. 8–16.
8. W. Klaiber, *Call and Response*, Abingdon Press, 1997, p. 97.
9. N. P. Moritzen, cited by D. Bosch, *Transforming Mission*, Orbis, 1981, p. 485.
10. Walter Brueggemann, *Biblical Perspectives on Evangelism*, Abingdon Press, 1993, p. 85.
11. S. Hauerwas and W. Willimon, *Resident Aliens*, Abingdon Press, 1989, p. 51.
12. Roland Allen, *Missionary Methods: St Paul's or Ours?*, Eerdmans, 1962, p. 3.
13. St Thomas's Church, Wincobank, Sheffield.

Chapter 10

1. George Lings, *Encounters on the Edge*, No. 18, the Sheffield Centre, 2003, pp. 11–12.
2. Michael Moynagh, *emergingchurch.intro*, Monarch, 2004, p. 196.
3. From the Aidan Liturgy in *Celtic Daily Prayer*, HarperCollins, 2000.
4. Prayer card from the Daily Office in *Celtic Daily Prayer*, Harper Collins, 2000.
5. Interview with Captain Martin Garner on 17 March 2003.
6. Council for Mission and Public Affairs, *Mission-shaped Church*, Church House Publishing, 2004, p. 74.
7. R. C. Tannehill, *Luke*, Abingdon Press, 1996, p. 152.
8. Vincent J. Donovan, *Christianity Rediscovered*, SCM Press, 1982, p. 81.
9. *Encounters on the Edge*, No. 18, 2003, p. 16.
10. Brian Stanley, 'Activism as mission spirituality: The example of William Carey', essay in Howard Mellor and Timothy Yates (eds), *Mission and Spirituality for Life*, Cliff College, 2002, pp. 72–6.
11. *Encounters on the Edge*, No. 4.
12. 'The Principles of the First Order of the Society of Saint Francis Day 16', cited by Brother Ramon, SSF, in *A Hidden Fire*, Marshall Pickering, 1985, p. 139.
13. *Encounters on the Edge*, No. 10, pp. 12–13.
14. Lesslie Newbigin, *The Household Of God*, SCM Press, 1953, p. 122.

Chapter 11

1. George Lings, *Encounters on the Edge*, No. 16, the Sheffield Centre, 2002, p. 12.
2. *Encounters on the Edge*, No. 16, p. 17.
3. *Mission-shaped Church*, Church House Publishing, 2004, p. 20.
4. Chris@Xcite, Oxford, questionnaire, 2005.
5. Nick Crawley, telephone interview, 1 June 2005.
6. Gordon Crowther, questionnaire, 28 June 2005.
7. Questionnaire, 2003.
8. *Mission-shaped Church*, p. xi.
9. *Mission-shaped Church*, p. 89.
10. First generation Quakers at Balby, late seventeenth century, cited by E. Arnold, *Why We Live in Community*, Plough, 1995, Preface.
11. This is where research such as that by George Lings and the Sheffield Centre, or Bob Jackson, might continue to prove extremely helpful for parishes and dioceses.

Further information and reading

Further research, information and advice

The Sheffield Centre for Developing Church Planting and Evangelism
Director The Revd George W Lings
Wilson Carlile College of Evangelism
50 Cavendish Street
Sheffield S3 7RZ
Tel 0114 272 7451

Anglican Church Planting Initiatives
Director The Revd Bob Hopkins
The Philadelphia Campus
6 Gilpin Street
Sheffield S6 3BL
Tel 0114 241 9560

Fresh Expressions
www.freshexpressions.co.uk

Courses in mission and evangelism including post-graduate courses

Wilson Carlile College of Evangelism
50 Cavendish Street
Sheffield S3 7RZ
Tel 0114 278 7020

Cliff College
Calver
Hope Valley
Derbyshire
S32 3XG
Tel 01246 582321

Index